MW00452248

BORDERLINE PERSONALITY DISORDER

TOOLBOX

A Practical Evidence-Based Guide to Regulating Intense Emotions

JEFF RIGGENBACH, PHD, LPC

BESTSELLING AUTHOR OF *THE CBT TOOLBOX*

ENDORSEMENTS

"Many people who struggle to acknowledge the presence of BPD traits in their lives continue to suffer needlessly. In the *Borderline Personality Disorder Toolbox*, Dr. Jeff Riggenbach explains this diagnosis clearly and offers a variety of skills from evidence -based approaches for treating it. This toolbox is a must-have for mental health professionals, people with BPD traits, and their family members."

-**Randi Kreger**,
Author, *Stop Walking on Eggshells* and *The Official Family Guide to Borderline Personality Disorder*
Founder, BPDCentral.com

"Written in clear user-friendly language, and drawing on vast research literature, beautifully summarizes what is known about BPD and how it can be effectively treated. Comprehensive in approach, it is an excellent resource for patients, clinicians, and families."

- **Joel Paris, MD**,
Author, *Treatment of Borderline Personality Disorder: A Guide to Evidence-Based Practice*
Editor, Canadian Journal of Psychiatry

"*Borderline Personality Disorder ToolBox* is a must-have comprehensive guide to understanding and managing BPD. Dr. Riggenbach's step-by-step accessible strategies will help the reader obtain empirically valid powerful tools to cope with Borderline Personality. This uniquely helpful guide will be an essential resource for both clients and their clinicians alike."

- **Leslie Sokol, PhD**
Distinguished Founding Fellow,
Academy of Cognitive Therapy, Fellow, ABCT
Co-author, *The Think Confident, Be Confident Workbook for Teens*

"Being asked to see a patient who has been diagnosed as having a Borderline Personality Disorder is enough to frighten even the most skilled and experienced clinician. Following Aaron T. Beck's notion of the "Continuity Continuum," Riggenbach describes and discusses the recommended treatments for various levels of Borderline, from mild to severe. This is a volume for every front-line therapist regardless of their professional discipline."

- **Arthur Freeman, EdD, ScD, ABPP**
Co-Author with Aaron Beck, *Cognitive Therapy of Personality Disorders*
Chair, Department of Behavioral Science, Touro College, NY

Copyright © 2016 by Jeff Riggenbach

Published by
PESI Publishing & Media
PESI, Inc
3839 White Ave
Eau Claire, WI 54703

Cover: Amy Rubenzer
Editing: Marietta Whittlesey
Layout: Bookmasters & Amy Rubenzer

ISBN: 9781683730057

All rights reserved.

Printed in the United States of America.

PESI
Publishing
& Media
www.pesipublishing.com

CONTENTS

JEFF RIGGENBACH, PH.D., LPC

Dr. Riggenbach is one of the most sought-after trainers and a recognized expert in the area of personality disorders. Over the past 15 years he has developed and directed CBT/DBT based Borderline Personality Disorder treatment programs at two different psychiatric hospitals serving over 500 clients with BPD. Over the past 10 years, he has trained more than 10,000 mental health professionals in various personality disorders seminars and CBT conferences. He also coaches people with BPD in non-clinical settings as well.

Dr. Riggenbach trained at the Beck Institute of Cognitive Therapy and Research in Philadelphia, is a Diplomate of the Academy of Cognitive Therapy, and is an international trainer on topics related to CBT, DBT and Personality Dysfunction.

His first book, *The CBT Toolbox: A Workbook for Clients and Clinicians* has been extremely well received and is being used in graduate programs as well as by mental health professionals and lay people alike. Dr. Riggenbach is known for bridging the gap between academia, research findings and day-to-day clinical practice, both in his workshops and writings.

"How is it that if Borderline Personality Disorder supposedly only affects 3% of the population that we always seem to find each other?"

Liz, an attractive, articulate 26-year-old asked me as she sat down in my office one day. "What do you mean?" I replied, knowing exactly where she was headed but awaiting the details anyway. She continued, "Last week, my friend Lindsay introduced me to a man named Eric. In the beginning, I was not attracted to him at all. After all, he was 20 years older than me, but the more time I spent with him that first evening, I increasingly felt like I'd known him my whole life.

"Our first date went so well that I called him back the next day and invited him over to cook dinner for him that night. I made us my variation of taco salad. The food proved delicious, and the meal was wonderful, in part because we shared fun, intellectually provocative conversation. We had a minor food fight and even took turns feeding each other. Dinner was playtime, as if we were children. Afterwards, I carried away our dishes and proceeded to wash them, cleaning up our food fight mess in between sinks full, subsequently returning to watch our first movie of the night, 'Stars Wars.'

"Sounds like a fun evening," I said.

"Wait, it got even better," she continued.

"As we watched the movie, Eric narrated in his radio voice persona, reliving his days as a disc jockey. I relished it. He had that quick wit that I fall for every time."

"It did get better. It sounds like you were having fun," I added.

"Until it got worse," she replied.

"He started out hilarious, but suddenly, he chose a dramatic, vulgar tone that made me uncomfortable and triggered my consciousness to quickly change. As I momentarily withdrew, he grew angrier and angrier so that he was enraged by the time my awareness returned. It happened so quickly, that I didn't even realize what had happened. In order to calm him down, I quickly initiated the one thing I knew would calm him: sex. Impulsive, guilt-laden, self-denigrating sex. It's always been my number one go-to to pacify guys.

"When it was over, he was crying over me, sobbing, begging me not to leave him, lavishing promises of change, excessive apologies and desperate pleas of me to forgive him and not leave him alone again as previous women had done. He felt bad for "guilting" me, and I felt responsible for the entire night's difficulties. He was afraid, and I, I was a self-loathing disaster. I followed his lead and apologized profusely as well. Afterwards, we hugged, made up, and decided to take a walk.

"As we walked in the crisp, fall night air, the tension now broken, the joking resumed. We walked briskly for about two hours, gaily bantering between ourselves, although I thought he enjoyed our time far more than I. The blaming, critical thoughts constantly running in the back of my mind prevented me from enjoying the fullness of our conversation and relaxing walk. As our time together concluded for the night, those same thoughts waged a war inside my mind." Liz paused a moment to breathe and steady herself for the remainder of her confession.

Knowing her and her patterns the way that I did, I suspected how this story might end, but asked her continue her tale.

"Upon my return home, I headed straight to my room, avoiding everyone. No eye contact; they'd know how shameful I had acted yet again. I knew I had to be punished, and so, I was ... by me."

Liz hesitated a moment, then looked up at me with a tear in her eye, and her tone turned in a slightly different direction.

Her mind had so easily overlooked the fun she had had earlier in the evening, choosing only to focus on the unhealthy choices she had made to engage in those risky and self-damaging behaviors. Despite knowing that the choices were all her own, they were all born from those horrible ideas poisoning her mind, a plague-like by-product of her Borderline Personality Disorder.

The further we explored this interaction with the two of them, it became apparent that she was right, and Eric had the same condition. He hated himself for how he had conducted himself that night. He apologized profusely. He begged for forgiveness, and pleaded for her not to leave him alone. Still, it was not enough for him... Unbeknownst to Liz, he went home that night and drank until he passed out because, "I couldn't bear the hatred I had for myself. I didn't intend to take advantage of her. I just got so enraged so quickly when her attention faded, so then, when she offered, I knew what I wanted in the moment. I never meant to hurt her."

Although Borderline Personality Disorder (BPD) is diagnosed three times more commonly in women than in men, it adversely affects the lives of millions of people all over the world. Roughly six million people in North America and 14 million people worldwide struggle with the disorder. It is more common than Schizophrenia and Bipolar Disorder. An estimated 10% of psychiatric outpatient populations and a staggering 20% of inpatient populations struggle with this diagnosis. Yet research and resources devoted to this condition continue to lag significantly and the condition remains somewhat misunderstood by primary care practitioners, the mental health community, and the public at large. Misdiagnosis remains common and quality treatment can be difficult to access.

While some stigma associated with the diagnosis remains, perception of BPD and its treatability has greatly improved over the last 10 to 15 years. Studies that are more recent have shown that the prognosis for most individuals with BPD is actually quite good. New treatments such as DBT (Dialectical Behavior Therapy), SFT (Schema Focused Therapy) and even some concepts out of traditional CBT (Cognitive Behavioral Therapy) have emerged – pioneering a new era in treating BPD, replacing age-old psychoanalytic ideas. One of the main themes of this book is that **There is Hope!** Many people with Borderline Personality Disorder, who find a competent therapist and are willing to put in the work, recover to a significant degree.

SO WHY ANOTHER SELF-HELP BOOK ON BPD?

REASON #1: The others are too complicated. Many books on BPD have been written by academicians who spend most of their lives in university settings doing studies funded by grants that require people to meet multiple requirements to participate in their research. By the time everyone has been ruled out for research purposes, there are often few left to benefit the "real world" person with BPD. Their language can often be so clinical or academic that it is difficult to understand what it means in plain English.

REASON #2: The others are often based on generalizations and stereotypes unfair to people who suffer from Borderline Personality Disorder. One of the themes of this book is that no two people with BPD are the same in every way. Many of the books portray the worst case scenario individual who is often depicted on shows like "Law and Order" where the character who supposedly has BPD kills herself and her three children. Many sick chatrooms exist that extend this image that represents few "real world" people with BPD. Although well intentioned, these often can have a harmful effect. Many people who have BPD that "looks different" see these horror stories they cannot relate to and assume they have something else and move on and never get the help they need.

REASON #3: The others are incomplete. Many "symptom management" approaches exist with the purpose of helping you "manage" your Borderline Personality Disorder or learn to behave better. We want you not only to behave differently but to feel better as well and accomplish not only surface level coping but meaningful change.

REASON # 4: The others are limited. A number of good self-improvement/motivational books for BPD exist that have been written by consumers from the perspective of the client with BPD. While this is a valuable perspective, it is only one side of the equation. Although many contain a legitimate viewpoint of Borderline Personality Disorder individuals who in some ways have overcome their symptoms, they are still often full of distortions in perception and generalizations based upon their specific experience and offer only one side of the equation.

This book is intended to give you a balanced overview of BPD. It is true that many times BPD is mischaracterized in the media, public opinion and by many mental health professionals themselves. Many people with Borderline Personality Disorder are charming, engaging, and genuinely want help for themselves and are willing to work very hard at their recovery. There are also people with BPD who blame others, aren't willing to work in therapy and engage in behaviors that are extremely hurtful to others. I have even had patients and their sick family members accuse others of horrible lies, including rape, in an attempt to damage someone they had a misperception of.

So whether you are a person who suffers from BPD yourself, a mental health professional, or a friend or a family member of someone with BPD, this book is intended to give you a balanced view of current research about the disorder. And more importantly, it is intended to give you some valuable tools to use with your provider that can help you overcome your BPD and take the next big step down your road to recovery.

A number of years ago, Paul Mason and Randi Kreger wrote a popular self-help book for friends and family members of people with Borderline Personality Disorder, *Stop Walking on Eggshells*. They describe results from three years of interviewing many people who had recovered from BPD. These are strikingly similar to the informal findings of my 10 years of running borderline personality disorder-specific treatment programming. Individuals with BPD who got significantly better had the following things in common:

 They took responsibility for their own actions. This is difficult for folks with BPD. Largely due to "blind spots" (which will be discussed later in the book), it is hard for many with this disorder to make the connection between their behaviors and the consequences of those behaviors. As such, learning from past mistakes is difficult and it feels like people just do things "to them" versus their choices contributing to the circumstances they often "find themselves in." This keeps many stuck in a victim mentality which keeps them from improving. Those who learn to take responsibility for their actions have a much better chance of recovery.

 They were willing to work through inner pain. It is easier to avoid really working through your issues. Some go to therapy with no intentions of being honest, especially when it is difficult to trust others. Some make superficial efforts, but continue to avoid the real work. Rather than feel the tough emotions necessary to feel to get better, they continue deflecting or dealing with pain through other means, such as alcohol, smoking pot, self-injuring, or some other "numbing" method that provides comfort in the moment, but keeps the person from true recovery.

 They had faith in themselves and believed God or others believed in their value. Borderline Personality Disorder at its core contains a belief that one is worthless, damaged, or defective. You will never meet a BPD sufferer who has healthy self-esteem. Learning to see value in oneself is essential for recovery from BPD. It is worth noting that most who come to believe this begin treatment believing this is NOT possible. Having a faith or important people in your life to help instill in your belief system that you have value and meaning is a powerful means for integrating that into your beliefs about yourself.

 They had access to continued therapy with a competent provider. A typical course of treatment for BPD is *one to four years*. Having a trained provider who is willing to stick with you through thick and thin is important. Progress is hard to come by for those who continually change service providers.

These are the common characteristics of those who improve from their Borderline Personality Disorder. I encourage you to keep them in mind and work to cultivate these characteristics as you pursue your own journey to recovery.

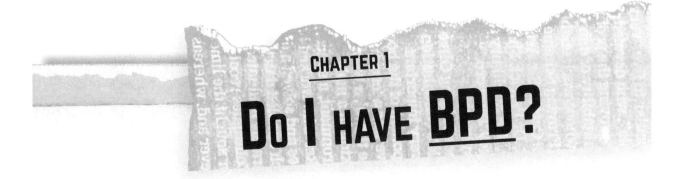

CHAPTER 1
Do I HAVE BPD?

There are many indicators a person may have BPD. There are also many checklists of this nature available in various resources. The problem is that the items on many of these lists may also be present in other types of problems. One thing that separates this from many other lists is these are *distinctly borderline behaviors and experiences*. The more of the following you identify with, the more likely it is that you have BPD.

 Do you often become terrified those closest to you will leave you?

 Do you notice a pattern in relationships of getting close to people quickly, but relationships ending abruptly and painfully? Multiple relationships end with hurt feelings? These may be observed in romantic relationships as well as family or friendship relationships.

 Have you ended relationships prematurely so others would not end them first?

 Can you meet someone, think they are the most wonderful person you have met, and soon be furious with them (hatred or disinterest)?

 Have you quickly taken on the values, hobbies, or behaviors of those around you rather than having stable, consistent things that you truly believe and enjoy?

 Do you feel like there is a "black hole" in you? A void that can seemingly never be filled?

 Do you feel lonely even when in a relationship or in a room full of people that in your "head" you know love you?

 Do you experience multiple intense mood swings in any one day?

 Do you have trouble being alone?

 Do you experience intense emotions related to guilt, self-hatred, self-loathing, or shame?

 Do you experience episodes of rage that are often followed by feelings of guilt and shame?

Have you injured yourself in some way in response to intense feelings of guilt or shame, or to make other intense emotions go away?

 Feel completely empty inside?

 Do you feel like contact with any person causes you too much stress?

 Have you cut off more than one person in your life by refusing to talk to them?

 Have you engaged in alcohol or drug use, promiscuous sex, binge eating, reckless driving, or shopping sprees in an impulsive manner in order to "numb out," feel better or create a "rush"?

 Done other risky things on the spur of the moment?

 Have you ever felt as though you did not even exist?

 Changing ideas about who you are? Career? Hobbies? Beliefs?

 Have you cut, burned, or otherwise hurt yourself *on purpose, but with no intent to die?*

 Have others accused you of being paranoid?

 Have you had periods of time you can't account for? Evidence you did something you don't remember doing?

FINDING A PROVIDER

Finding a provider who is competent to treat Borderline Personality Disorder can be difficult. Many clinicians lack education about the disorder. Some may be able to recognize it, but do not know how to treat it. Still others may have an "old school" mentality about the disorder and believe that it is "untreatable" or have other misconceptions about the condition. Some may have beliefs about the diagnosis that make it impossible for them to effectively treat BPD. You may find the following suggestions helpful in locating a provider who is best for you.

1. DO YOUR RESEARCH. Look at what clinician reviews say. Find his/her provider profile online. Those clinicians who have a list of what they "specialize in" that lists 50 things likely do nothing well. Find someone who is specifically knowledgeable about Borderline Personality Disorder.

2. GET REFERRALS. Talk to other people with BPD. See which providers they have found helpful. Talk to other people without BPD who have sought therapy for another reason. Competent therapists typically know other competent therapists. Even if that person's clinician does not specialize in treating BPD, they likely will know another provider/treatment facility in the area that does.

3. ASK QUESTIONS. Interview potential therapists. Some may do this on the phone. Others may require you to come in and pay for an initial visit. It is worth it to find someone who you believe is qualified and who you may be able to develop a trust in to work with. A good "fit" is just about as important as someone who is highly qualified. Some important questions to ask might include:

Do you treat people with personality disorders? How many people with BPD have you treated?

It is obviously preferable to have someone who has some familiarity with the disorder. Some may say they treat BPD, but they only have worked with one or two people with the diagnosis. If they have limited experience treating the diagnosis but are in a peer consultation group with others who have, this can be helpful as well.

 How do you conceptualize BPD? In a nutshell, what can you tell me about what this condition is?

Make sure the therapist does not just think BPD is "complex PTSD." As will be discussed in the etiology section, many people with BPD don't have trauma in their backgrounds. Even if you do have a background that includes trauma, treating PTSD and treating BPD are very different. Also make sure the clinician does not just think it is a variant of bipolar disorder. Ensure they view BPD as a distinct diagnosis and that they have a method of treatment specifically for it. Screen out any potential therapist who attempts to steer you away from the diagnosis or wants to call it something else.

 What type of treatment approach do you use with BPD?

This is a piggy back off of the last question. Bipolar disorder is treated primarily with medications. PTSD is treated primarily with exposure and response prevention, grounding and other management strategies. Make sure they have a clear treatment approach for BPD. Effective treatments for BPD include Dialectical Behavioral Therapy, Cognitive Behavioral Therapy, Schema Focused Therapy, and Mentalization-Based Therapy. Make sure the person doesn't say a version of, "I'm eclectic – I use a mix of things with different people." Usually being "eclectic" means they don't have specific training in anything. There are very specific approaches to treating BPD and having a structured, intentional approach is important. You do not want someone who does "a little yoga and a little art therapy."

 What can you tell me about the research in the area of BPD?

Most clinicians probably won't be able to cite research off the top of their heads, but you can often get a sense by their answer if they are competent enough to have a general idea of what is going on in the area. They should know one of the modalities mentioned above has been demonstrated to be effective and be able to tell you something about your prognosis. When I went on medical leave, one of my clients' insurance companies required her to see a clinician who knew nothing about the research, was not interested in helping her monitor her target behaviors, and instead insisted she use his model that required her to punch his fist and yell profanities (not once asking about her destructive behaviors).

 What are your qualifications?

This question is not designed to elicit the specifics of where they went to graduate school or where they finished in their class. The best academics are not necessarily the best clinicians. The particular license they hold is not even that important (although in general, social workers tend to have a broader education but less actual therapy training than psychologists, LPCs, or LMFTs). You are looking for any specialty training they have. Professionals who have an interest in treating BPD have generally sought out some advanced training or specialty certification in an approach proven to treat BPD. Those who have gone out of their way to receive additional continuing education on a particular population often have a "heart" for those people and they likely may have more interest in working with you and be more invested in your recovery.

Do you believe people with BPD can get better? Have you treated people with BPD who have improved? Can you tell me in what ways did they improve?

It is obviously important that the clinician believes people with BPD can improve. If you have Borderline Personality Disorder, you may not believe you can improve. You may have unsupportive family members who do not believe you can improve. If the clinician in question has a proven track record, even better! If they have seen and helped other BPD patients improve, they will believe you can improve. You don't need a therapist who sides with your hopelessness on your down days. Finally, listen for how they answer the questions, monitor their non-verbal communication, and assess for yourself if this is a person you could see yourself working with.

WHAT DOES THE RESEARCH SAY?

Dialectical Behavior Therapy (DBT) is the most empirically supported form of treatment for Borderline Personality Disorder. It is the most popular, and it is quickly becoming the most commonly requested form of treatment. DBT now has 9 randomized controlled clinical trials for BPD specifically and many other trials (over 30) researching co-occurring problems with BPD, isolated symptoms of BPD, or other associated features of the disorder. It is well documented that DBT does what it sets out to do: modify specific behavioral targets associated with BPD. DBT has been demonstrated repeatedly to decrease self-injurious behaviors, decrease suicide attempts, decrease admissions to psychiatric hospitals, and decrease overall days in the hospital. So we know DBT to be a highly effective form of treatment.

It is, however, important to note, that being the most empirically supported form of treatment does not mean that it has been compared repeatedly against other modalities and been shown to be superior. It simply means it has been studied the most frequently. Traditional CBT has some good studies, Mentalization-Based Treatment has shown some promise, and schema therapy probably has the most impressive studies of all, although there have only been three from this approach. So we need to see these studies replicated before drawing any significant conclusions. Actually the largest study ever done on individuals with Borderline Personality Disorder, involving 13 different countries, is currently underway and is from a schema therapy perspective. The upcoming results will be interesting to monitor.

The bottom line is that research related to BPD continues to mount, although slowly. We continue to learn more about the essential "ingredients" of these treatments. While there is still much to learn in this area, much has been discovered, particularly in the last 15 years. Common factors in successful treatment of BPD that have been identified include:

1. A TREATMENT AGREEMENT/CONTRACT.

If your provider is not asking you to sign some kind of a treatment agreement or contract, it likely is not BPD-specific treatment. An agreement or contract is a crucial component of successful treatment for this condition. You need to know what the expectations are before you know what they are asking you to commit to. If you are a person with BPD, you likely have had problems with boundaries in your life. The contract is step one towards modeling how to operate within a framework of "rules." We don't like to say it this way, but all relationships have "rules." Most are probably unwritten, but all relationships have rules. Even if the notion of signing an agreement makes you shudder, know that it is in your best interest even if it feels restricting.

2. A TRUSTING THERAPEUTIC RELATIONSHIP.

It is all but impossible for people with BPD to improve outside the context of a trusted therapeutic relationship. All people with Borderline Personality Disorder have trust issues. Some are minor; some have full-blown paranoia. But all people with BPD have had people they could not count on in their past.

Trusting someone requires vulnerability, which is inherently difficult for people who have been hurt. But you will not come to believe that you are worthwhile and that others can be faithful/loyal/not leave you without gradually being willing to let your walls down. Occasionally (but very rarely) people with milder cases can find a sponsor, a trusted coach, or even a healthy and nurturing romantic relationship that can foster similar changes.

3. VALIDATION.

People with BPD feel like nobody else can understand them, like no one knows where they are coming from. It is true that most have not had the exact experiences, so few can know exactly what it is like to have this disorder. Due to these past experiences and the extreme emotions experienced in adulthood as a result, it is important for people with BPD to feel heard. . . to feel like their experiences from the past or emotions in the moment are heard, acceptable, and to some degree understood. Approaches that are only directive and challenging in nature do not work.

4. A METACOGNITIVE COMPONENT.

Even before mindfulness was all the rage, the ability to notice one's thoughts and behaviors was an important feature of successful treatments of BPD. In order to challenge dysfunctional or distorted thoughts, one must first be able to recognize what thoughts they are having, label them as thoughts, and then demonstrate the ability to "do" something different with them. More contemporary forms of mindfulness, mentalization, and acceptance-based approaches place less emphasis on even changing thoughts. They will want you to learn to "just notice" thoughts and learn to detach from them. Whether the modality actually wants you to learn to think differently over time or not, an ability to recognize and describe one's thoughts is vital.

5. PRESENT DAY PROBLEM-SOLVING VERSUS AN EMPHASIS ON EARLY CHILDHOOD EXPERIENCES.

In the same way that overly challenging or confrontational approaches are not helpful with BPD, styles that never confront will not succeed either. Approaches that sit back and say "hmmmmm – I'm wondering why you are curious about that," or wanting to remain focused on what happened before you were five rather than answering your questions or taking a more direct approach to problem-solving with you are not helpful either.

6. SKILL BUILDING.

This is what this book is all about. It has taken the best of the tools from the most evidence-based approaches and described them in one, practical, easy-to-use workbook. Use these with your therapist or by yourself in between sessions to continue to build your mastery over intense emotions so that you can feel better, make more effective decisions, and live the life that you desire!

CHAPTER 2

THE BPD DIAGNOSIS

Borderline Personality Disorder is actually one of 10 of what *The Diagnostic and Statistical Manual of Mental Disorders, 5th Edition®* [or DSM-5®] (APA, 2013) calls "personality disorders." A personality disorder is technically characterized by a *pervasive and enduring pattern of inner experience, behavior, and cognition that deviates markedly from the individual's culture.* These patterns begin at an early stage of development, are e*nduring and inflexible,* and lead to significant clinical distress or impairment. The DSM–II described personality disorders as "ego-syntonic."

The term ego-syntonic is not used in the current DSM and has not been for many years. When the DSM–II came out in 1968, Freudian psychoanalytic/psychodynamic thought still dominated the psychological landscape. Much of this theory has now been shown to be flawed (the evidence supports very little of these initial ideas) and current DSM language is **atheoretical**, meaning the criteria are descriptive in nature and do not use language from any one psychological *theory.* Although outdated, this term **ego-syntonic** came from the Freudian concept of the "observing ego." Freud said this group of individuals lacked the ability to "step outside themselves and observe their own behavior objectively." [Comer, 1988] We might say they have, "poor insight." Perhaps you have heard the term "blind spots" in personality - parts of our personality we have difficulty seeing in ourselves that others are able to see. Although all people have these "blind spots," for individuals with personality disorders, these spots are typically much larger. So behaviors often are not seen as a problem by the individual with BPD but are viewed as a problem by significant others in their lives. Thus developing this initial insight that is lacking in many is a crucial first step to recovery from Borderline Personality Disorder (as well as any other personality disorder).

Flexibility is a key component of what is considered an **adaptive** personality. John Oldham used the phrase, "the magnificent variety of non-pathological behaviors." People who have flexibility in personality are able to 'be different in different situations,' or wear different 'hats' depending upon what the circumstances call for. For instance, they are able to be assertive if someone makes an unreasonable request, but they are also able to be submissive if someone in authority is ordering them to do something. They are able to be fun and spontaneous at social events, but serious in business meetings or funerals. They can have sufficiently high standards without being unreasonable. They can be organized and tidy when the situation calls for it, yet flexible and let the kids mess up the house while opening presents on Christmas morning. Individuals with personality disorders tend to be more rigid. However their particular sets of traits predispose them to "be", they have difficulty being any other way. Thus, they end up being **maladaptive**, or not working well in certain settings, because the same way to be does not work in every setting. Behaving the same way in an amusement park that you do at a funeral does not work in both settings. Thus, another major goal for the personality disordered individual is to learn to develop some flexibility.

The term **enduring** means that these traits are stable over time. If you have a personality disorder (and you have developed a little insight), you will be able to see these behaviors having begun in early adolescence (or before) as you look back on your life. Nobody develops a personality disorder for the first time at age 30. We will discuss some differential diagnosis considerations at the end of this chapter, but often people may experiment with a substance, go through a time of grieving after a divorce, or any other temporary life stressor and develop some qualities that look like personality disordered behaviors, but these are not grounds for a diagnosis if these are not patterns that have persisted over time.

Finally, this definition includes patterns of inner experience, behavior, and cognitions that pose significant emotional distress. *Perception* is a term that refers to how one receives information. How we "hear" things or perceive things is filtered by our beliefs/cognitions. When these are distorted, we view things in extreme and skewed ways that lead to intense emotions and oftentimes disagreements with others who do not view situations in the same way. Intense feelings and unstable relationships often accompany personality disorders. Due to the varying nature of different types of personality disorders, individuals with different diagnoses perceive themselves and others differently.

 People with **Narcissistic Personality Disorder** overestimate their own importance, abilities, etc. and often dismiss, diminish, put down, or belittle others.

 Those with **Dependent Personality Disorder** have difficulty even voicing appropriate disagreements with others and view themselves as incapable.

 Individuals with **Histrionic Personality Disorder** overvalue physical attractiveness and undervalue other qualities in themselves and others.

 Those with **Obsessive-Compulsive Personality Disorder** have issues with perfectionism and place unrealistic value on orderliness, being on time, and doing things "the right way." They live their lives in a state of perpetual annoyance and frustration due to their unrealistic expectations of others and themselves.

 People with **Antisocial Personality Disorder** violate social norms, laws and other people. They have little to no empathy, they lack remorse for any of these violations, and they can be violent.

 Individuals with **Paranoid Personality Disorder** believe others are out to get them or hurt them in some way when, in reality, they are not in danger.

So the specific perceptual errors are different with each specific disorder, but the role of perception distorts how these people view themselves, others, and society and that has a profound impact on their feelings (inner experience) and behaviors. This is just a glimpse of a few of the core issues of personality disordered individuals. Borderline Personality Disorder is just one of the 10 disorders and it is characterized by a very specific type of maladaptive (unhealthy) thinking and behaving.

Before we get to the BPD criteria, a quick word on the difference between a "trait" or a "feature" and a "symptom." A symptom is defined as "a departure from normal functioning, noticed by the patient, reflecting the presence of an unusual state or disease." A trait or feature has to do with a characteristic or attribute that makes someone or something unique. The short of it: A symptom is always a bad thing, a trait or a feature is not. You probably never want a bloody nose, high blood pressure, or to have a panic attack. Suspiciousness, however, can be a good thing (adaptive). If you work in the CIA or for Homeland Security, some degree of suspiciousness can serve you well. If you don't work for Homeland Security, but you believe you do, you are delusional! If you tell people you do, but you know that you really don't, you are a psychopath. If you don't work in a setting like this and you believe everyone is out to get you, your suspiciousness is out of control and the paranoia is considered dysfunctional. So when you hear the terms symptoms vs. traits, know that traits can be more or less helpful based upon the context a person is in, and if harnessed in an effective manner, can actually be strengths. And know that you probably never want a symptom if you can help it.

Limits to categorical models. Personality disorders are currently classified using what is called a categorical model. This means that if you meet the identified number of criteria, you have the disorder. If you don't, you do not. There isn't much room for grey. The reality is that most people do not have an obvious personality disorder or nothing at all. Most people have more or fewer of these traits. It is also somewhat subjective to identify what we mean when we say a person "meets criteria." DSM-5 requires that an individual meet 5 of the 9 criteria to be diagnosed with the disorder. In the real world, few people meet all 9 criteria strongly. To further illustrate the problem, one person could meet all 9 of the 9 criteria in a very mild way; so technically, he qualifies for the disorder, but may be very high functioning. Another person could meet only 4 of the 9 criteria, but meet the 4 that she does meet very strongly and be a very sick individual, yet technically not even qualify for the diagnosis. Like any other diagnosis, you can be "a little BPD" or "severely BPD." There are different sub-types. There are different levels of severity. There are different manifestations in different people. So, practically, what this means is that *BPD looks very different in different people.*

There has been a movement for a number of years to characterize personality disorders drastically differently than we do now. These models are called dimensional models, which also have some pros and some cons. Many believed dimensional models were going to play a much more significant role in DSM -5 in terms of how we characterize personality disorders. However, the work group failed to incorporate these concepts in a helpful way for people in the clinical setting. Some of this *trait-specific methodology* was put in section 3 of the DSM-5 as an area for further research, so they can be referenced by people curious to know what these changes were proposed to look like. The five factor model is among the most popular dimensional model for those who have an interest in further research. Just be aware that future versions of DSM may describe these conditions differently. But this will not mean that our current models are not valid. Don't think, "Oh they had it all wrong – what I read before is no longer relevant — maybe I don't have this." These are just academic people attempting to make the process more scientific.

BPD CRITERIA MADE EASY

Most people who have had this diagnosis even mentioned to them, whether it has been confirmed or not, have gone onto the internet and read these criteria. This clinical lingo, however, is very often not fully understood by individuals or family members curious to discover if this is in fact the condition they are dealing with. Here are these criteria, with detailed explanations of what they mean, accompanied by "real world" manifestations. Read them carefully. Many find it a useful exercise to rate each criterion on a scale of 0-10, where zero means "I don't see any of this criterion in me," and 10 means "this criterion describes me perfectly." This is obviously somewhat subjective as well, but at the end of the exercise, you will have a decent idea of how many criteria you likely meet and how strongly. This is usually a conversation best had with your psychiatrist or therapist. Also because of the "blind spots" previously referenced, it may be helpful to have someone who knows you well answer how they view you on a scale of 0-10 in each area.

BPD DESCRIPTIVE ADDITIONAL FEATURES – DSM-5

The latest version of the DSM-5 adds the following descriptive language for Borderline Personality Disorder: A pattern of self-undermining just prior to goal completion (i.e., dropping out just prior to obtaining a degree, having an affair just prior to wedding or engagement, etc.).

FRANTIC EFFORTS TO AVOID REAL OR IMAGINED ABANDONMENT

As mentioned above, people with BPD can have many combinations of these diagnostic criteria; inasmuch, many people with BPD will not have many of these. But this abandonment criterion is met by just about everybody with BPD. The majority of individuals with BPD have some version of thoughts constantly running through their minds that significant others in their life will leave them, or that they won't be there to meet their needs. This manifests differently in different people. In an attempt to ensure that they are not left, many people will constantly call or text a loved one needing seemingly constant reassurance that the person they are concerned with is committed to being emotionally supportive and not leaving. Although the BPD individual usually does this out of fear, it is often perceived by significant others as "smothering" or being overly needy and tends to be experienced as energy draining by the significant other. Thus, people who experience abandonment in this manner may frequently find themselves "freaking out" at incidents that are small or meaningless to family members or friends. Not having a text returned "soon enough" and misinterpreted "put downs" are frequent triggers for these episodes. **For these individuals, being alone proves quite difficult, if not emotionally painful, and minor separations can be experienced as traumatic.**

Some people with BPD have experienced that feeling of rejection so painfully in the past, they make a decision to "put up walls" and never let anyone in. This does not mean social isolation or never leaving the house, as is common for someone with clinical depression or anxiety disorders. Many people with Borderline Personality Disorder have very good social skills on the surface level. It's just when others get too close that feelings get intense and relationships get volatile. One can be quite gregarious and very good socially without actually connecting with other people. It is even possible to be sexually promiscuous and not actually attach emotionally. By doing so, these individuals protect themselves from ever experiencing intense rejection ever again. However, they also rob themselves of the benefits of any connection, authenticity, or meaningful relationships.

Other individuals with BPD engage in what is known as overcompensation. These people "see the writing on the wall," whether it is really there or not, but that is their legitimate perception. They often think, "I am going to dump him before he can dump me," and may engage in other sabotaging behaviors. Over-compensators like the feeling of being in charge ("It feels better in the moment if I dump you rather than waiting until you dump me"), but later regret it because their actions continue to ensure that they will end up alone. Individuals who experience abandonment in this way commonly describe feeling interpersonally slighted, or "getting their feelings hurt" in situations or in response to comments that would not make others feel this way. Any disagreement is often viewed as rejection and feels deeply personal due to this abandonment "filter" that colors how comments are interpreted.

One final characteristic of abandonment in BPD is that loss is often experienced in a prolonged and profound manner. Grieving in response to a death or the ending of a significant relationship is emotionally painful for everyone, but for many people with the abandonment-related Borderline Personality Disorder quality, the grieving process can be quite complicated and many are prone to getting stuck in it.

Based upon this description, do you see this in yourself? If so, how do you see this in yourself? If you are having this conversation with a family member or friend, do they see this in you? If so, how strongly?

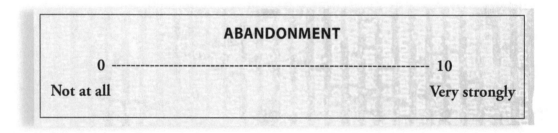

_____

_____

_____

A PATTERN OF INTENSE RELATIONSHIPS CHARACTERIZED BY
ALTERNATING BETWEEN EXTREMES OF IDEALIZATION AND DEVALUATION

Cognitive therapy has language you might have heard called black and white thinking or "all or nothing" thinking. The fancy cognitive therapy term is dichotomous thinking. This is very similar to the psychodynamic term "splitting." Whatever you want to call it, the BPD individual has a pattern of thinking that involves these extreme polarized interpretations. When we idealize someone or something they are "all good." When we devalue someone or something they are "all bad." This extreme thinking style in relationships leads to chaotic, intense relationships. Individuals with Borderline Personality Disorder (and their partners) will often report, "When the relationship is good, it's really good, but when it's bad, it's really bad." One of my patients said in group one time, "*I put my boyfriend up on a pedestal until he pisses me off, then I yank the pedestal out from under him and beat him with it.*"

This is a common characterization of the BPD relationship. Relationships start out very quickly and become intense almost immediately. "I jump in all the way too early," said another patient. Again, this can vary with the subtype, but most individuals with BPD have difficulty moving at an appropriate pace. When they meet a new person of interest, they spend (or attempt to spend) extraordinary amounts of time with them in person, calling, texting, facebooking, etc. They commonly have sexual encounters almost immediately and may move in with a new significant other only weeks after meeting them. This inability to move slowly creates an "instant intimacy" in relationships, clouding their judgment immediately. Statements like, "I think he's my soul mate," and, "I feel like we've known each other our whole lives," are common even after meeting someone the first time. This inability to see negative qualities initially often gets people in unhealthy relationships quickly. Following a date that ends in physical or sexual involvement, the BPD individual often leaves thinking they are in love and it is a sign of a deep meaningful relationship, and then when the other doesn't reciprocate, that person is seen as a user, perpetuating the BPD person's belief that others are untrustworthy and that he/she will always be abandoned. One BPD patient described it this way:

> "*Trust proves tricky for me. Perhaps I seem to trust strangers, divulging intimate details of my life too quickly only to be hurt. When I do this, maybe I am unintentionally self-sabotaging because I feel worthless/unlovable/undeserving, maybe I am intentionally sabotaging myself as a form of emotional self-harm, maybe I am testing my belief that all people are untrustworthy, or maybe I just need to tell someone because I've kept it to myself for so long and need to feel heard. On the other hand, perhaps I trust no one—because I have been betrayed and hurt too intensely in the past.*"

Relationships fluctuate dramatically with regard to attitudes and feelings towards others people. Significant others can go from "the best ever" to "the worst ever" overnight and then back again the next day. "I love him and he is my soul mate" quickly becomes "I hate him and he is pond scum" all in the same day.

This pattern often ensues until the non-BPD individual can't stand it and leaves, reinforcing the abandonment belief.

Due to this, it is not uncommon at all that individuals with Borderline Personality Disorder have been married 3+ times and have had multiple dating relationships / sexual encounters in between. Occasionally, people with BPD will be married to the same person for 20 years, but that single relationship takes on that same 'black and white' quality. It is very stormy, chaotic, and "off and on" again. Somebody is always threatening to leave, but never really does. Or they leave for three days, but always come back. Conversations that for most couples pose disagreements which are solved in 30 minutes turn into energy draining conversations that leave both parties exhausted late into the night. Occasionally, then, this dynamic will show up within the context of one relationship, but often it is multiple relationships.

Typically, these "unstable relationships" are thought of within the context of romantic relationships. However, this pattern can show up in other personal relationships, family relationships, friendships, and even professional relationships. It is not uncommon for people with BPD to have had 3, 10, or even 20+ therapists!

Because of this, BPD individuals live a life of extremes – everything is black or white – they have difficulty dealing with grey areas, and difficulty even seeing middle ground. Not only does this make it difficult to establish reasonably well-balanced opinions of others and to cope with relationships, it also creates problem-solving deficits. Decision-making can be quite difficult if all you have to choose from is two extremes. The middle ground alternative that may prove to be the most effective choice is not even viewed as an option, so it never gets tried. Significant others or professionals are often needed to help the BPD individual generate "middle ground" options to choose from.

Based upon this description, do you see this in yourself? If so, how do you see this in yourself? If you are having this conversation with a family member or friend, do they see this in you? If so, how strongly?

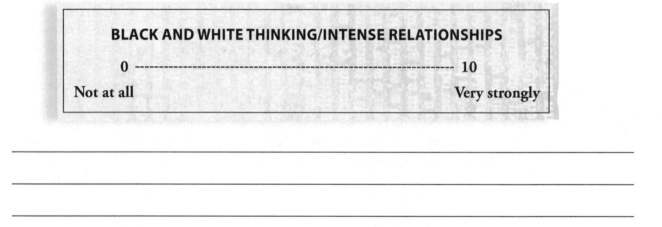

BLACK AND WHITE THINKING/INTENSE RELATIONSHIPS

0 --- 10

Not at all   Very strongly

_____

_____

_____

IDENTITY DISTURBANCE

I recently had a patient in my office for an initial assessment. I asked her a question that, for many of my patients, is the simplest of all the intake questions to answer: "What do you do for fun? What are your hobbies?" She responded, "I have no idea who I am, what I like, or if I'll ever have a place in this world."

These types of statements are common for people with Borderline Personality Disorder who struggle with identity disturbance. Some people read this criterion on the internet or in a self-help book and believe this relates to low "self-esteem." A lot of people have low self-esteem but don't have BPD. Identity disturbance in the BPD individual is associated with a much deeper sense of not knowing who one is. This may show up in confusion with regard to sexual preferences. Significantly more individuals with BPD endorse same sex attraction than their non-BPD counterparts. For some people it may show up instead in terms of occupational preference.

It is also not uncommon for people with BPD to have changed their majors multiple times, not knowing "what they want to be when they grow up," even if they are 45 years old. After entering the workplace, many people with BPD jump from job to job to job and have difficulty maintaining stable employment. This usually has nothing to do with competence. Many people with BPD have higher than average IQs. Relational conflicts are common on the job, and some people with BPD quit for those reasons. However, many people with BPD do a job for a period of time and just get bored and quit. They just have difficulty finding something that sustains their interest for an ongoing period of time. They get excited about something for a while and then they get bored. For some people, this identity criterion manifests in terms of frequent changes to physical appearance. Multiple tattoos, body piercings, and/or frequently changed hair color may be ways this manifests in different individuals.

Because of this lack in core identity, people with BPD are often overly susceptible to environmental influences. If someone seems critical, you feel awful; if somebody praises, you feel wonderful for the moment. If a friend suggests you do something that evening, you likely will agree. When I ask the question, "What do you do for fun?" another patient responded, "*I never really have had any hobbies. I never really knew what I liked, so I have just always kind of been like the chameleon doing what everybody else wanted me to do. I used to mountain bike because my boyfriend did, but once I broke up with him, I haven't done it since. I also used to be a part of a knitting club because two of my friends from the job I had at the time were in it. But now that I am not hanging out with them anymore, I haven't knitted since – and I don't miss it a bit.*" Some patients with BPD even struggle with core values or existential or religious beliefs. These can seem to fluctuate from moment to moment as well.

It is important to recognize that is a quality of BPD and is NOT a sign that you have no values. It usually just means that you are less solidly anchored to the values than some.

Another patient described this manifestation for her in the following way:

> "*Having BPD does mean that I have an unstable identity. You may notice my instability when I conform to the interests of you and others involved in my life. I may change who and what I like and want because I do not know, because I feel unlovable/ worthless/ bad/ undeserving of my own feelings and interests, and because I desperately want to belong somewhere, anywhere in life. I am doing it so that I can be someone I believe is worthy of friends, family, and life. I am not manipulating you; rather, in these times, I am emulating you because I want to be like you, you are important to me.*"

So although identity struggles of some kind are common in people with Borderline Personality Disorder, these show up in drastically different ways in different people. Any behavior that might be considered developmentally-appropriate for adolescents, but not for 45-year-old adults, may be commonly manifested. This is simply another demonstration of how no two people with BPD are alike in every way.

Based upon this description, do you see this in yourself? If so, how do you see this in yourself? If you are having this conversation with a family member or friend, do they see this in you? If so, how strongly?

IDENTITY RELATED ISSUES

0 --- 10

Not at all   **Very strongly**

IMPULSIVITY IN AT LEAST 2 AREAS THAT IS POTENTIALLY SELF-DAMAGING

This is a characteristic of BPD very few people with the diagnosis don't exhibit. Again, the type of behaviors may vary, but impulsive decision-making or behaviors often accompany this disorder. Impulsive substance use, sexual promiscuity, binge eating, shopping, reckless driving, and spending sprees are common manifestations in most individuals with BPD. Many describe needing a "quick feel good." When you don't trust others and you don't have the means to create peace within yourself, it makes sense to seek comfort from some external source. People with BPD commonly look for something external they can do to themselves to influence their internal feeling state. Impulsivity may also take place within the context of relationships (i.e., impulsive decisions to shut down, lash out, break up, move in together, etc.).

As a result, people with Borderline Personality Disorder may often have co-occurring substance use disorders and eating disorders. Sexually transmitted diseases, unwanted pregnancies and multiple abortions are often sources of shame that accompany the disorder as well. Financial and legal problems may be additional unwanted consequences of impulsive behaviors.

Because these behaviors often serve the function of alleviating intense emotions, they often follow rejection or other hurtful interpersonal reactions. Occasionally these behaviors are engaged in out of boredom. Thus, as the BPD individual becomes more skillful at handling interpersonal interactions and creates a life they enjoy, the triggers for these impulsive behaviors often slowly evaporate.

Finally it is worth mentioning that this is one of the two criteria that often leads to a misdiagnosis of bipolar disorder. See the differential diagnosis section at the end of this chapter to better understand the differences before rating yourself in this category.

Based upon this description, do you see this in yourself? If so, how do you see this in yourself? If you are having this conversation with a family member or friend, do they see this in you? If so, how strongly?

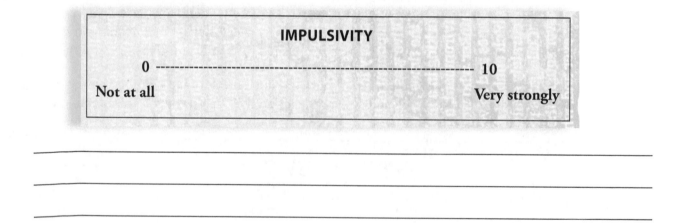

IMPULSIVITY

0 —————————————————————————— 10

Not at all   Very strongly

_____

_____

_____

RECURRENT SUICIDAL BEHAVIOR, GESTURES, THREATS, AND SELF-MUTILATING BEHAVIOR

This one encompasses a lot. It sometimes helps to break this down into three categories: *Parasuicide, chronic suicidality,* and *acute suicide.* Parasuicide is intentional self-harm with no intent of dying. Another term you will hear to refer to this is *self-injurious behaviors or SIB.* Cutting is the most common type of self-injurious behavior, but there are many ways people with BPD may choose to hurt themselves including burning, head banging, skin picking, and other methods.

It is important for friends and family members to realize that most self-injurious behaviors are not suicide attempts in the BPD person's mind. Their intent is not to die. Most BPD individuals who engage in parasuicidal behavior are doing it as a coping skill, not a suicide attempt. They don't want their life to end; they just want the emotional pain to end. Because of this, these events are typically not best characterized as "suicide attempts." It is also important to note that, although the motivation for these behaviors is not to die, many times self-injurious behaviors may result in accidental death. So even if a friend, family member, or health care professional understands that the individual's motive does not involve a wish to die, it is important to recognize that these behaviors still pose significant risk. In addition to accidental death, infections and other medical complications can result from parasuicidal behavior.

So if the motive of self-harming is not to die, then what is it? Well, there is not one *IT.* Actually eight motivations for parasuicidal behavior have been commonly given by individuals with BPD as to why they hurt themselves.

Consider the following motivations and check the boxes that apply to the reasons that you can relate to:

☐ **To make one's anguish known to others.** People with BPD suffer intense emotional pain, incomprehensible to the general public. Many are used to hearing things like, "you look so cute, you are so smart, you look fine, and there should be nothing wrong with you." For some people with Borderline Personality Disorder, self-harming behaviors are a way to *externalize internal pain.* "When people see blood running out of my arm, then they can see how much I really hurt and how sick I really am," one of my patients explained. This is a common expression for people with BPD.

☐ **To end an argument.** Some people simply say, "If I hurt myself, he/she will get off my back/ stop criticizing me." This is probably less common but self-harming behavior can just serve the function of ending a fight or disagreement when it has reached the point where the person cannot handle any more stimuli.

☐ **To elicit a sympathetic response.** Here is the one "attention-seeking" motive. As we have covered, people with BPD have often felt invalidated during their childhood. Many have learned over the years that one way to get validation or caretaking responses is by self-harming. It is a natural instinct for most caring people when they see someone hurting/bleeding, etc. to come and help them or take care of them. While these responses intuitively seem "right," and feel good to the person who sought them out, it is important to note they are actually counterproductive to recovery. Caring responses to unhealthy coping attempts continue to reinforce them. The BPD individual interested in recovery will work with his/her therapist and support system to develop alternative ways to get the responses they need.

☐ **Numbness.** "I'd rather feel something than nothing," and, "I'd rather feel physical pain than emotional pain," are common statements from people with BPD. Self-injurious behaviors can serve this function for some clients as well.

☐ **To improve problem-solving.** This motive is probably less common as well. But some people with BPD will describe a sense of clarity of thought after self-harm; "like my head clears up and I have a better sense of what to do," one patient described. One of my male BPD individuals said, "It's just kind of like I reach up and hit reset on the video game – like I get to start over."

☐ **Revenge.** Some people with BPD engage in self-injurious behaviors as a means of getting back at someone. Many with BPD have punitive schemas or beliefs that influence them to frequently engage in behaviors seeking revenge. Self-harming can be one such way to do so, as it can be upsetting to loved ones.

☐ **Anxiety reduction.** This may be the most common reason for parasuicidal behaviors. Research is still being done in this area, but there is something different in the biology of individuals who can cut themselves and have it feel good versus most people who cut themselves and it hurts. The answer to this probably lies in the endorphins, but the verdict still seems to be out. Endogenous opioid receptors are one area of current research that is theorized to be involved. Many people with BPD will experience a "release" or a sense of "relief" when cutting or self-harming that gives them a temporary "high." It is also worth noting that some people will engage in excessive body piercing and/or tattooing for this same reason. A portion of individuals with BPD will describe the same sensations as a motive for continuing these behaviors as they serve the same function but are more socially acceptable in some circles.

☐ **Self-punishment.** Some people simply believe that they are bad and deserve to be punished. In these individuals, self-harm follows some act that serves as "evidence" that they are a bad/worthless person who deserves to be punished. Once they have self-harmed, they have "gotten even" with themselves or the "debt has been paid." Individuals who self-harm for this reason are rarely attention seeking and should not be treated in this way. These people typically hate themselves in a deep and profound way.

Hopefully you were able to identify some motives for your behaviors if self-harming is an issue for you. Remember, this is all in the category of *parasuicide*.

Chronic Suicidality has to do with longstanding thoughts of suicide, even if residing in the back of one's mind and even if the individual has no immediate intent of acting on them. People who have struggled with depression and had bouts of major depressive episodes, will often have suicidal thoughts with those episodes. Major depressive episodes can have their onset at any age (but often not until adolescence or adulthood) and often accompany a specific life stressor (divorce, lost job, death, etc.). Conversely, people with chronic suicidality usually remember thoughts of wanting to be dead at very early ages. Some will even report these thoughts as early as age 4 or 5. Children of that age usually don't fully understand what it means, but will remember thoughts of "wanting to go away," or "just not be here." Also individuals with chronic suicidality describe these thoughts as "always sort of in the back of my mind" and "like as soon as anything stressful happens those are the first thoughts that creep into my mind." These thoughts are usually passive, meaning they are easily dismissed and do not accompany a plan of action or intent to act. Thoughts of this nature are NOT grounds for hospitalization. If BPD individuals went in the hospital every time they had a fleeting suicidal thought, they would spend their lives in institutions and never learn how to cope with them. Parasuicide and chronic suicidality are unique to BPD.

Acute suicidal thoughts involve immediate death. These thoughts consider specific ways to kill oneself and involve intention to follow through with suicide plans. These thoughts are not unique to people with BPD. Patients with bipolar disorder, clinical depression and others may have these thoughts. Acute suicidal thoughts frequently require hospitalization, particularly if the person experiencing them is unable to firmly commit to a safety plan.

Based upon this description, do you see this in yourself? If so, how do you see this in yourself? If you are having this conversation with a family member or friend, do they see this in you? If so, how strongly?

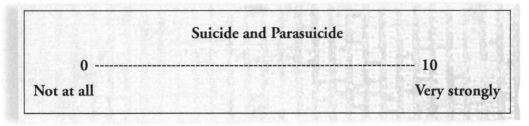

_____

_____

_____

AFFECTIVE INSTABILITY DUE TO MARKED REACTIVITY OF MOOD

This is fancy terminology for mood swings. Research consistently shows that people with Borderline Personality Disorder are hyperactive to emotional stimuli. What does this mean? It means they are easily triggered. It means things happening around them affect their moods in a much more profound way. That is one reason it is difficult for people with BPD to be each other's support system. Hearing about stressful things happening in the lives of people they care about is often too difficult for them to handle. This mood swing in the BPD individual is different than the type of mood swing experienced by the patient with bipolar disorder. BPD mood swings are almost always relationally triggered, and they involve immediate intense feelings. Individuals with BPD don't feel emotions everyone else doesn't feel. They just feel them more intensely than others do. If they are mad, they are really mad. If they are upset with themselves, they really hate themselves. If they are anxious, they are very anxious. When they feel down, they experience profound sadness. One of my patients said, "I just feel everything big!"

An important aspect of this worth noting is that these "mood swings" that involve down swings in mood that are often experienced as "depression" by the individual with BPD are really very different than the type of clinical depression that is improved by medication. More on this later, but this type of situational mood swing is not significantly affected by medication. Also because these swings are environmentally triggered, a person with BPD can have multiple "mood swings" in one day, depending upon what is happening in that person's life. So it is not uncommon at all for a person to be irritable in the morning, happy by lunch, and deeply hurt and furious by dinner. One of our patients showed a sense of humor with this when she showed up to group with a t-shirt that said, "Caution – Next Mood Swing – 6 Seconds!"

Although anything can trigger these swings, research has also established that people with BPD consistently misread others. BPD individuals consistently misinterpret facial expressions and facial features. Again this can be accounted for by a combination of beliefs that influence perceptions and underlying biological factors in the areas of the brain responsible for this type of sensory processing.

Based upon this description, do you see this in yourself? If so, how do you see this in yourself? If you are having this conversation with a family member or friend, do they see this in you? If so, how strongly?

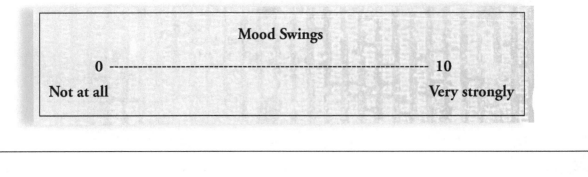

_____

_____

_____

CHRONIC EMPTINESS; FEELINGS OF EMPTINESS

This one is fairly self-explanatory. For people who experience this, no further explanation is necessary. One of our patients calls this her "black hole." Another refers to it as "my vortex of misery." The bad news is that this is also the criterion that improves the most slowly and, in some people, does not seem to dissipate at all over time. We have many patients who have made significant improvement in eight of the nine areas, but still routinely say things like, "I am in a room full of people in my head I know love me but feel completely alone." Sometimes this emptiness is also experienced as depression, but it is also unresponsive to medication. Perhaps this is due to lack of depth of interests, being easily bored or finding few things in life that fulfill them. It has also been compared to that feeling most people feel when going through a cycle of grief following the death of a loved one, divorce, or some other significant loss. Many people wake up with a "sick feeling in their gut" that comes in waves when remembering something related to the loss. Some even describe not just an emotional response, but a visceral feeling in their abdomen. This resembles the emptiness that the BPD individual feels every day of their lives.

Based upon this description, do you see this in yourself? If so, how do you see this in yourself? If you are having this conversation with a family member or friend, do they see this in you? If so, how strongly?

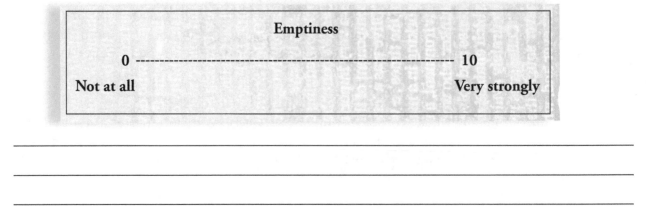

_____

_____

_____

EPISODES OF RAGE

This one is also fairly self-explanatory. And this one is the criterion BPD individuals usually have the best insight into. They know whether or not they explode on people. This should not be mistaken for everyday irritability or annoyances that anyone can feel. Irritability seems to be a symptom of almost every psychiatric disorder (and can even be experienced by people who have never been diagnosed with any mental illness in their lives). BPD episodes of rage are intense and immediate. One of our clients said, "I'm going to explode and I don't care who gets hit by the shrapnel." As with many of the other impulsive or destructive behaviors, consequences take a back seat in the "heat of the moment." Verbal aggression, physical fights, and temper tantrums may all be manifestations of this rage.

Sometimes these behaviors are engaged in "to make sure others care" or they may be punitive in nature ("to do to others what has been done to me so they can feel what this is like").

Based upon this description, do you see this in yourself? If so, how do you see this in yourself? If you are having this conversation with a family member or friend, do they see this in you? If so, how strongly?

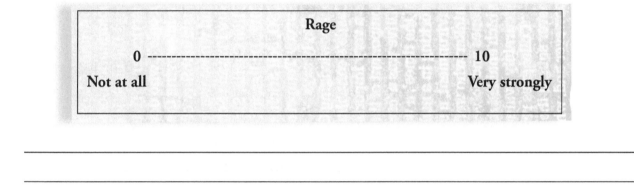

_____

_____

_____

TRANSIENT STRESS-RELATED PARANOID IDEATION
AND SEVERE DISSOCIATIVE SYMPTOMS

Let's break this down. Transient means brief. It comes and it goes. Stress-related speaks to the trigger. When arousal is high (so when you are really angry or really stressed out) one or both of the following may occur:

Paranoid ideation. Ideation is a fancy word for thoughts. This is typically not a psychotic type of paranoia, such as someone with schizophrenia is likely to experience. (e.g., thinking the FBI is following them, alien beings are coming to kidnap them, etc.). This is what might be called an "everyday paranoia." People who exhibit this type of paranoia simply misinterpret real life events that really do happen. They believe when they see two people talking, "they are probably talking about me," or they expect others to behave badly toward them even though they know they love them.

Dissociative Symptoms. Everyone dissociates a little bit. Dissociation could even be viewed as happening on a continuum. Have you ever been driving along a route you are familiar with and looked out the window and realized you just missed your exit? Have you ever sat through a sermon in church or a lecture in class and then when you left, you were not able to tell someone what it was about? So everyone "zones out" a little from time to time. However, people with BPD tend to do this more under stress than most. Not all people with Borderline Personality Disorder experience this. Some may never fully "lose time," but may have times of feeling "spacey" during which time their recollection of events is vague. They may get in a fight with a significant other and before they know it they are yelling things they later honestly do not remember saying.

Some people with BPD do struggle with severe dissociation and lose larger portions of time and may even meet criteria for co-occurring dissociative disorders.

Based upon this description, do you see this in yourself? If so, how do you see this in yourself? If you are having this conversation with a family member or friend, do they see this in you? If so, how strongly? With regard to this criterion, it is often helpful to rate paranoid thinking and dissociation separately, as many people experience one but not the other, and they are really two completely different phenomena lumped into one criterion.

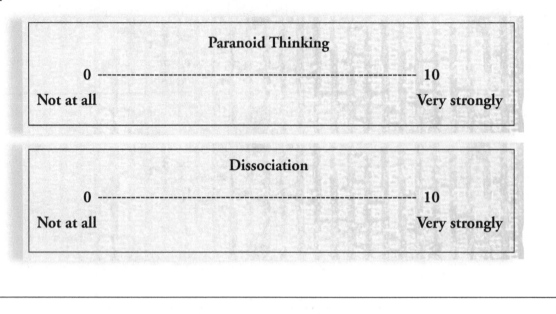

UNDERSTANDING *MY* BPD

Hopefully you now have a better understanding of the criteria. However, one of the most consistent concerns we hear patients in our program voice is that, "We aren't all the same." This is one of the most important things friends, family, and even professionals don't understand about individuals with Borderline Personality Disorder. Like any other medical condition, you can have a severe case of something or you can have a mild case of it. You might get a severe sinus infection, or you might have a mild one. You can have diabetes that is type I or type 2. You can have a severely broken bone or a mild fracture. Similarly, some people have a mild version of BPD, some a more moderate one, and some severe. Depending upon the combination of criteria you meet, your condition may look drastically different from that of someone else who also meets the criteria. There are different severity levels and different subtypes (see the Professionals section for a breakdown of the subtypes). Depending on the type of impulsive behaviors you engage in and the number of criteria you meet for other personality styles, your presentation may differ. Understand *your* condition inside and out. Know your manifestations. Know your triggers. Learn the best skills for managing your version of this condition. The upcoming tools were designed specifically to help you achieve that goal.

It is true that there are many different "versions" of BPD. It is also true that BPD gets misdiagnosed often. David Robinson (not the former NBA player with the Spurs, but the Canadian psychiatrist) notes in his book *Disordered Personalities* that in its less obvious forms, BPD can be a challenge to diagnose. Between the inherent difficulties in making this diagnosis, and the lack of education on personality disorders, it is unfortunately not an uncommon experience for people to have received multiple diagnoses (which may or may not have been accurate) prior to receiving the diagnosis. Use Robinson's diagram to note how BPD can have many overlapping manifestations with other conditions.

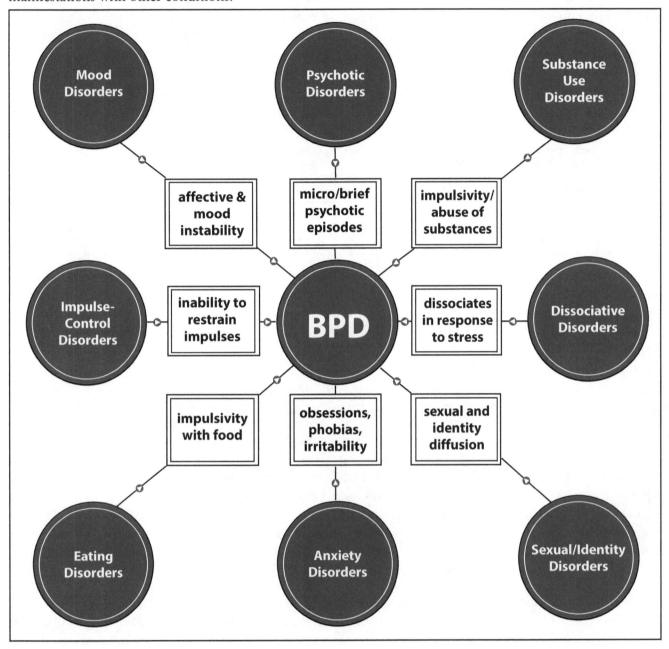

As illustrated above, because BPD has an affective (mood swing) component, it is not uncommon for people to be diagnosed with bipolar disorder. Because the swings sometimes involve downswings, people are often diagnosed with depression. Because mood swings can involve anxiety and panic attacks, patients with BPD are often diagnosed with anxiety or panic disorders. Due to the impulsive behaviors that often accompany BPD, patients may be diagnosed with an impulse control disorder. Because the impulsive behaviors can involve alcohol or drugs, clients may be diagnosed with a substance use disorder. Due to the sexual and identity diffusion, BPD individuals may be diagnosed with a sexual or gender identity disorder. Because impulsivity can involve binge eating or other issues with food, some may have eating disorder diagnoses. Due to the dissociation under stress previously described, occasionally dissociative disorders are diagnosed. Finally, due to the brief psychosis under stress, occasionally psychotic disorders are diagnosed.

Possibly the most common diagnostic error clinicians make is giving a bipolar disorder diagnosis when the patient actually has BPD. Criterion 4 (impulsive behaviors) and 6 (mood swings) are the two most likely culprits. One problem is that criterion 4 for BPD lists the exact same types of behaviors (impulsive substance use, spending sprees, promiscuous sex, binge eating, reckless driving, etc.) that the DSM-5 also lists for a manic episode in a person with bipolar disorder. If a person really does have a bipolar condition and only engages in these behaviors during the context of a manic episode, those behaviors should not be attributed to BPD. As stated above, BPD impulsive behaviors typically come in response to a relationship issue and serve the function of regulating intense emotions. Secondly, a "bipolar mood swing" can be differentiated from a "borderline mood swing" with relative ease by someone trained in the disorder. The following simplified table illustrates 3 key points of emphasis we ask our clients to pay attention to.

Bipolar Mood Swing	BPD Mood Swing
Biological trigger	Environmental trigger
Involves neurology/energy	Involves real human emotions
Longer duration of swing	Shorter duration of swing

Research has suggested that stress in general can induce a manic episode. It does not take research for one to conclude that stressful circumstances in general can "bum a person out." However, there is no specific environmental "mania trigger." If you have bipolar disorder and someone says, "I think that dress makes you look fat" that might be rude, but it doesn't trigger a "manic episode." People misuse this term all the time. "He pissed me off so I got all manic and went and did all these crazy things." That is not how mania works. That *IS* how BPD episodes get triggered, though. Comments "push your buttons" and emotions fly high immediately. Secondly, "bipolar mood swings" are affected by a person's neurology. People will say things when they start to get manic like, "I feel 'happy' or 'euphoric' or 'excited'," but it is just because they have elevated energy levels.

Conversely, a person in a depressed state will say things like, "I feel sad or down, or lethargic," but it's just because they don't have any energy! Simply put, bipolar disorder is about energy up vs. energy down. It doesn't involve guilt and shame, hatred, and panic. It has nothing to do with abandonment. It isn't because you are upset over a relationship. It is because your neurology is experiencing a swing. If you are going two or three nights without sleep and you feel good, that is not BPD. If you can't get out of your bed for 3 weeks because your body feels like it just does not have the energy - that is also not BPD. Finally, consider how long your swing lasts. Bipolar spectrum related swings can last weeks or months. BPD swings usually last hours, and the person has a much quicker return to baseline (especially if something positive happens in their life).

There are a few possible reasons that clinicians have been historically reluctant to make a personality disorder diagnosis. Many clinicians are uneducated on personality disorders. It is typical for most Master's level programs to have one psychopathology course and one section of this is devoted to personality disorders. A second reason may have to do with payment for treatment. Some insurance companies are improving, but traditionally many payor sources have been reluctant to cover treatment for personality disorders. Subsequently, overworked clinicians who are bombarded with paperwork to meet bureaucratic standards and stressed to meet productivity requirements hurriedly diagnose only conditions they can bill for so as not to be hassled by administrators.

Additionally, since you can't really medicate a personality disorder, medically-oriented psychiatrists and other prescribers may be more prone to diagnose a condition they can medicate (because that's all they do). As one of my previous medical directors was fond of saying, "If all you have is a hammer and you're not dealing with a nail, you are kind of screwed." Finally, and perhaps most commonly, mental health clinicians have become so politically correct and fearful of "labeling" a patient that they incompetently choose not to document a medically-appropriate diagnosis.

Although co-occurrence is low, it is possible to have both bipolar disorder and BPD.

It should be noted that not all of these diagnoses have to be incorrect. It is possible to meet criteria for BPD and legitimately meet criteria for one or more other diagnoses. In fact, 90% of people who qualify for BPD do meet criteria for one other diagnosis. Actually, 80% meet criteria for two or more other diagnoses. So occasionally people with BPD are *misdiagnosed* with something they don't really have. But more often, they may actually meet criteria for one of the other diagnoses, and perhaps that is how they are in that moment, so the clinician identifies the manifestation, but misses the core condition responsible for the behavior. These are actually easy mistakes for uneducated clinicians to make, especially considering the fact that many people with BPD do, indeed, present differently at different times.

SYMPTOMS OVERLAP WITH OTHER PERSONALITY DISORDERS

It could also be noted that borderline personality disorder has symptoms that overlap with those of other personality disorders. For instance, similar to the dependent personality disordered individuals, people with BPD are triggered specifically in relation to being "alone" or left in relationships. As with the histrionic personality disordered individual, physical appearance can play a disproportionate role in self-esteem to the person with BPD. Suspicious cognitions, particularly under stress, can mimic paranoid personality disorder. Impulsivity associated with BPD can take the form of law-breaking behaviors (shoplifting and related offenses can be common in one BPD subtype), similar to antisocial personality disorder. Some individuals with BPD lack empathy, a quality shared with a narcissist. Finally, some with BPD exhibit perfectionistic tendencies, which can overlap with the obsessive-compulsive personality disorder.

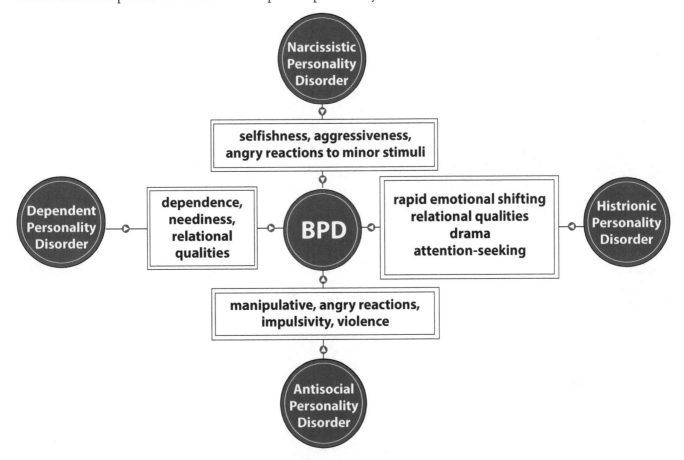

The bottom line is that BPD can look like a lot of other things. An accurate diagnosis is necessary before treatment can target relevant symptoms and features. Until this occurs, positive treatment outcomes are nearly impossible.

Get to know *your* BPD. Find a competent and trustworthy clinician to help you. Recovery is possible. The first step is developing an understanding of exactly what you have.

CHAPTER 3

WHERE DOES BPD COME FROM?

When wrestling with BPD, many people wonder, "Where the heck did I get this from?" We don't completely know. I will give you a little background information, but this book is less about where it comes from and more about what to do now. Psychology has long been guilty of offering theories as to why something came to be, but offering few answers as to how to move forward and what to do to make it better. Even if we knew the exact cause, it would be of little benefit if we had no answer for what to do next. We do know that BPD is five times more common in first-degree relatives. This could be related to a genetic predisposition being passed down, or it could mean behaviors are being modeled.

For reasons not completely understood, people seem capable of developing BPD in different ways. Since there appear to be multiple pathways to borderline personality disorder, answering the "why" questions is complex. No one factor can fully account for the development of BPD. Most research now supports some version of what is known as the diathesis-stress model, which suggests that biological predispositions increase vulnerability to be adversely influenced by environmental events. So it is really an interaction of biological and environmental risk factors.

For clarification, a *risk factor* increases the likelihood a person will develop a certain condition, but does not *cause* it or guarantee a person will get it. For instance, a traumatic event (often times abuse) is *causal* for PSTD in a way abuse is not causal for BPD. It is not possible to develop PTSD without some traumatic event (often abuse) but there are people who develop BPD who do not report early life trauma or something they would call abuse. **The good news is that, just because we may be predisposed to something, does not mean we have to get it.** For instance, many may have a predisposition for lung cancer, but if they choose not to smoke, they don't get it. Others are predisposed to diabetes, but if they monitor diet and blood sugar, and keep their weight under control, they likely do not get it. Some people may have a predisposition for alcoholism, but if they do not drink, they won't become alcoholics.

So, in the nature versus nurture discussion, BPD appears to be fair combination of the two. Learning there are biological factors as well as psychological factors seems to make this diagnosis less mysterious and more acceptable to the public in ways that were not the case even as recently as 10 years ago.

If we are talking about a combination of biological factors and environmental factors, what are the biological factors? Biosocial geneticists are people who attempt to separate out heritable aspects of personality from learned aspects of personality. They have developed what they call genetic concordance rates, or heritability rates, for each personality disorder. Heritability rates for BPD have been estimated between .44 and .69, depending on whose studies you look at. Therefore, this means that likely at least half of your BPD is biological in nature.

Other biological findings include neuroimaging studies that show there is a neural basis of the disorder. EEGs have shown that individuals with BPD have abnormalities pointing to pathology in the prefrontal cortex, causing impairment in executive functioning, which is associated with impulsivity – and physiological abnormalities in the neural systems that regulate emotional activity, impulse control and cognition. Studies have also shown bilateral decreases in the hippocampal and amygdala volumes when compared to non-BPD individuals. This heightened activation of the amygdala could account for why people with BPD are hypersensitive to environmental stimuli, and could contribute to "emotions overpowering thoughts" when these people get upset.

> **A quick side note**: This does have some implications on what tools to use and when. When your arousal is high (and your amygdala is overpowering the prefrontal regions of the brain), grounding emotion regulation skills, and other behavioral tools will probably prove most helpful. Your mood has to be in a more level place to engage in the more thinking (cognitive) tools.

While some biological differences have been observed with BPD, it is important to remember that we also know that the environment affects the brain as well. Traumatic and stressful events influence long-term changes in neural pathways, so a person's biology as an adult may be different than it was when he/she was born.

There are also a number of environmental risk factors for BPD. Childhood physical and sexual abuse is common in the backgrounds of many people with this condition. Although they would not necessarily consider it "abusive," many people with BPD describe early separations, loss, inadequate parenting, or lack of nurturing as children. While some people with BPD have horrific abuse in their background, others describe things such as frequently being compared to a sibling or what might be considered milder versions of harmful parenting. What Marsha Linehan described, in a way that no one had previously articulated, was that regardless of what *actually happened* in their respective childhoods, all people with BPD report feeling invalidated – and having internalized the message that no one cared about them.

Linehan described three different types of invalidating environments:

1. **THE "CHAOTIC" FAMILY** – This family always has some kind of "drama" going on. Often there is substance abuse in the family. Financial problems are common. Abuse or other volatile communication styles often characterize this family. Parents are so caught up in their own dysfunction that children's needs often go unmet.

2. **THE "PERFECT" FAMILY** – This is the family that must appear perfect to the outside. In these families, it is more important how things look than how things really are. Image protection is valued at the cost of the well-being of its members. Parents cannot tolerate negative emotional displays from children. "What happens in the family stays in the family," thus it is not acceptable to seek help. Children are often treated as victims and sympathy is expressed towards them, but there is no way out.

3. **THE "TYPICAL" FAMILY** – This family expects its members to appear "normal." Cognitive control over emotions is emphasized and it is not OK to express feelings. A member's worth is performance-oriented and based on what they can master/accomplish.

These are common backgrounds of people with Borderline Personality Disorder. It bears repeating that many people who are exposed to these same environmental factors do not develop BPD. The more severe the genetic risk, the less environmental risk is required. The less severe the genetic risk, the more severe the environmental risk is required to develop the disorder. So, it is likely that some critical combination and interaction (the more emotionally dysregulated the child, the more invalidating responses they are prone to evoke from parents) is necessary for BPD to develop.

Several factors contribute to *degree of impairment* related to BPD symptoms. For those who have been abused, the severity of abuse, types of abuse, and age of onset of the abuse all have a direct correlation to how severely BPD features may manifest.

In summary, genetic risk factors interact with life events to contribute to the development of BPD. And it is less important how something became a problem than knowing how to solve the problem. The next part of this book is a compendium of tools to help you.

TOOLS INTRODUCTION

Nobody likes for their environment to have power over their emotions and for their mood to be largely dependent upon what others say or do or how others treat you.

Wouldn't it be nice if you didn't feel so helpless and at the mercy of your emotions? So how does one gain this sense of empowerment? By getting a toolbox full of skills complete with a manual of how to use them!

You may remember that learning skills is one of the common factors related to overcoming BPD. Until people with this diagnosis acquire healthy tools, the only coping skills they often have for modulating their emotions involve using some external aid (alcohol, drugs, sex, spending, binge eating, etc.) to influence their internal feeling state. The more tools you have in your toolbox that you learn how to use effectively, the less reliant you will be on external "feel goods" to influence your mood back to a tolerable state.

You might have caught the line "that you have learned to use effectively." Having a complete set of tools does little good if one does not know how to use them effectively. You can have the best hammer in your toolbox, but if you are using it when your project calls for a screwdriver, you likely won't get the result you want. Similarly, if on your camping trip you are sleeping on your charcoal and using your tent to try to light a fire, you will also have little success. In the same way, assertiveness is a great tool to learn, but if you attempt to use it with the homeland security agent because you don't want to take your shoes off at the airport security checkpoint, it probably won't end very well for you. So you see it is not only important to develop these skills to have in your toolbox … it is also necessary to know what skills to use and when.

Never fear! This book is your guide to all things tools related! The tools are divided into seven sections: Motivational tools, Dialectical Behavior Therapy (DBT) tools, Cognitive-Behavioral Therapy (CBT) tools, crisis management tools, relational tools, Schema Focused Therapy (SFT) tools, and other tools.

So here comes the "meat & potatoes" of this book. Learn these skills. One by one. See which skills work for you. It should be noted that the same tools don't work for everyone. Skills that work well for others in your BPD treatment program may not work for you. Also you may find that a certain tool that worked for you once, may not always work. Just because a given tool doesn't work during one attempt to use it doesn't mean you should toss it aside never to be considered again.

Most people find it helpful to pick a list of 10 (or so) "go to" tools that work some of the time for them, so in moments of distress they have a menu of options to choose from, and likely at least one of those 10 will help in any given episode. Make notes for yourself: Which skills work for what type of episode? Do certain skills work best to extinguish a panic attack? Are other tools better when you are in a rage? What skills are most helpful when you notice yourself starting to dissociate? When you feel like engaging in risk-taking behaviors that in the moment you couldn't care less about (but you will likely regret in the future)?

Learn the skills. Learn how to use them. Learn when to use them. And gradually start to enjoy the freedom that comes from no longer being a prisoner to your emotions.

CHAPTER 4

MOTIVATIONAL TOOLS

Some motivational speakers get paid $25,000 a day. Why?

1) Because they are overpaid.

2) Because MANY people struggle with motivation.

Some people are more interested in being different than others. Likewise, some people with BPD can be "self-starters" while others need a little extra incentive to get moving. For those of you in this category, here are a few motivational tools to help you get started.

The Miracle Question

What would your life look like if you started to achieve some of your goals? How specifically would you be different? It is helpful to know where we want to go before we start the journey.

Steve de Shazer, a family therapist who wrote primarily in the 70s and 80s, asked his patients the following change-provoking question. I thought it might serve as a useful first tool. It is difficult to give directions to someone who does not know where they want to go.

If you were to wake up tomorrow and were granted a miracle and all your problems were solved, what would be different?

_____

_____

_____

Now that you've given a general answer, perhaps it is helpful to think about how you'd like your life to be different in these specific areas:

How would I like my physical health to be different?

_____

How would I like my mental health to be different?

_____

How would I like my relationships to be different?

_____

How would I like my spiritual life to be different?

_____

How would I like my finances to be different?

_____

How would I like my occupation/volunteerism to be different?

_____

Copyright 2016 © Jeff Riggenbach, _The Borderline Personality Disorder Toolbox_. All rights reserved.

YOUR READINESS FOR CHANGE

Change can be difficult for people with BPD. First, one has to have insight that certain behaviors are problems. Then, consistency is needed to follow through. Millions of Americans make New Year's resolutions every year to lose weight. Most don't lose weight. Why? Because setting goals is easier than actually making changes. Many people have good intentions; few have good follow-through. When making a change of any kind, all humans go through the following stages. Take notes as you desire, and answer the questions that follow. This tool can help assess your readiness for change.

One area of my life I need to make a change in is:

_____

_____

_____

_____

_____

_____

One change I am committing to make is:

_____

_____

_____

_____

_____

Stages of Change Theory
(Developed by: Prochaska & Diclemente)

Potential Relapse

Precontemplation

↓

Contemplation

↓

Preparation

↓

Action

↓

Maintenance

I believe I am currently in the _____ stage shown in the Stages of Change Theory.

I am willing to take the following steps to move to the next stage _____

_____

Copyright 2016 © Jeff Riggenbach, *The Borderline Personality Disorder Toolbox*. All rights reserved.

Expressions of Concern

What is a problem for us is often not a problem for other people, and things that are problems for them are oftentimes not a problem for us. Review the following questions and consider the validity of the concerns others have expressed.

Has anyone in particular expressed concern about your behaviors? _____

_____

What particular concerns have been expressed? _____

_____

Which ones do you dismiss? Why do you dismiss them? _____

_____

Which ones do you take seriously or see where they are coming from? _____

_____

How could you see that they might have some validity? _____

_____

How do you decide if a concern shared is worth changing your behavior? _____

_____

Copyright 2016 © Jeff Riggenbach, *The Borderline Personality Disorder Toolbox*. All rights reserved.

GOAL SETTING

Leslie Sokol says, "Vague treatment goals lead to vague treatment outcomes." Goal setting can be difficult for people with BPD. Often, surviving the moment is hard enough. Looking into the future can seem unmanageable. Goals can be short-term, intermediate, or long-term. Short-term, intermediate, and long-term goals all play an important role in success.

For the purpose of this exercise, a **long-term goal** will be anything that will *take at least 1 month and possibly years* to achieve. An **intermediate goal** can be anything achievable in *one day to one month*. A **short-term goal** will be considered anything you can accomplish t*oday*.

For instance:

Long-Term Goal: Run a 5K in 3 months

Intermediate Goal: Lose 8 pounds this month

Short-Term Goals: Walk 1 mile in park today and eat 2000 calories or fewer today

There are a few important questions to ask when setting good goals for yourself:

- Is my goal attainable?
- Is my goal realistic?
- Is my goal measurable?
- If I accomplish this goal, how will it help me?
- What could get in the way of accomplishing my goal?
- What is the smallest step I could take today that would move me toward my long-term goal?

Spend a few minutes to develop some goals for yourself. For each long-term goal, consider what intermediate and short-term goals may be necessary to help you achieve it. Remember your self-care plans. Goals can be physical, emotional, relational, spiritual, occupational, or other.

Examples of Good Goals

Physical:

Run a race, play tennis or golf again, walk around my neighborhood 5 out of 7 days, lose 10 lbs, lift 50 lbs, bench press 100 lbs, take a nap, take only one dose of anti-anxiety medicine per day.

Emotional:

No binge eating this week, reduce my self-harm behaviors to 1 per week or 1 per day, not have sex when so-and-so calls, continued abstinence from substances or gambling, journal three times per week, complete one thought log per day, practice mindfulness once per day, use three distraction techniques today, yell at my spouse one time or less this week.

Relational:

Call a friend, set a boundary, have coffee with someone, say "thank you," confront someone attempting to take advantage of you, write a letter, break up with an unhealthy boyfriend/ girlfriend, send an email, say "no," go to a social event with a friend, go on a date, work on

Copyright 2016 © Jeff Riggenbach, *The Borderline Personality Disorder Toolbox*. All rights reserved.

forgiving someone, don't answer the phone when someone calls when it is in your best interest not to talk to that person, apologize, try a new event to meet new healthy people.

Spiritual:

Pray, meditate, go enjoy nature, read the Bible or other spiritual writings, go to church or synagogue, fellowship with like-minded believers, sing or listen to worship music.

Occupational:

Take a class, update your resume, take a vacation, confront a co-worker appropriately, study 30 minutes/day, set alarm and get up as if you were going to work before you actually have the job, cut out want ads in the newspaper, practice for interview, read book/article in your field, network even when not working.

My Goals:

_____

_____

Long-Term:

_____

_____

Intermediate:

_____

_____

Short-Term:

_____

_____

One small step I will take today to move toward my goal is:

_____

_____

Copyright 2016 © Jeff Riggenbach, *The Borderline Personality Disorder Toolbox*. All rights reserved.

CHAPTER 5
DBT Tools

Dialectical Behavior Therapy (DBT) tools were developed specifically for people who struggle with challenges we now know to be related to BPD. DBT tools, when applied in a specific way and in the right situations, can be some of the most valuable tools for helping people with BPD.

DBT treatment programs are divided into 4 modules:

- Mindfulness
- Emotion Regulation Skills
- Distress Tolerance Skills
- Interpersonal Effectiveness Skills

Marsha Linehan, credited with the creation of DBT, was a big believer in acronyms to help people remember skills. Avid DBTers will notice in the following acronyms: IMPROVE, ACCEPTS, DEAR MAN, GIVE and FAST (you'll see them identified in the tool titles with some larger capital letters).

IMPROVE for ways for improving the moment

> **I** – Imagery
>
> **M** - Meaning
>
> **P** - Prayer
>
> **R** - Relaxation
>
> **O** – One Thing
>
> **V** - Vacation
>
> **E** - Encouragement

ACCEPTS for considering some ways of distracting

> **A** - Activities
>
> **C** - Contribute
>
> **C** - Compare
>
> **E** – (change) Emotions
>
> **P** – Push Away
>
> **T** - Thoughts
>
> **S** - Sensations

DEAR MAN is a guideline for objective effectiveness

> **D** - Describe
>
> **E** - Express
>
> **A** - Assert
>
> **R** - Reward
>
> **M** - Mindful
>
> **A** – Appear Confident
>
> **N** – Negotiate

GIVE is used for developing relationship effectiveness skills

> **G** - Gentle
>
> **I** – Interest
>
> **V** – Validate
>
> **E** – Easy Manner

FAST is the acronym for developing self-respect

> **F** – Fairness
>
> **A** – (no) Apologies
>
> **S** – Stick (to your values)
>
> **T** – (be) Truthful

Get Validated!

"You shouldn't feel that way."

"It doesn't really hurt."

"Pull yourself up by your bootstraps and buck up."

"There's no reason to feel depressed; you have so much to be thankful for."

Any of these types of comments ring a bell? Cognitive therapist Bob Leahy said, "Not every person is ready to change, but everyone is ready to be validated."

For many individuals with BPD, their background consisted of a pattern of invalidating messages. Regardless of what actually happened, every person with BPD experienced feeling invalidated in some way. Emotional invalidation can be defined as occurring any time a person's emotional experiences are rejected, ignored, or judged. Conversely, emotional validation is the process of learning about, understanding, and expressing acceptance of another person's emotional experience. Use the following tool to identify people in your life who could provide that validation and places you could meet further people to validate you.

People currently in my life who could validate my feelings and experiences are:

    1. _____

    2. _____

    3. _____

If I don't have anyone currently in my life who I believe could validate me, places I could find new people are:

    1. _____

    2. _____

    3. _____

One small but reasonable change I am willing to make this week to increase my feelings of validation is:

_____

_____

_____

_____

Copyright 2016 © Jeff Riggenbach, *The Borderline Personality Disorder Toolbox*. All rights reserved.

MINDFULNESS

Do you ever feel so overwhelmed with your own thoughts and feelings that it seems as though you are your worst enemy? Mindfulness allows us to gain awareness of our thoughts, feelings, and the things around us and helps us to find calm in the storm. **By learning not to judge these, but merely to be aware of them, we can learn to be less reactive and to respond more effectively in the moment to what is happening.**

Mindfulness is specifically defined as *"paying attention to something, in a particular way, on purpose, non-judgmentally"* (Kabat-Zinn, 1990). While there are a multitude of mindfulness exercises out there, and many books devoted to nothing else, let's just have you start with a simple introductory exercise based upon this definition.

Pick something to pay attention to. It could be:
- Your breath
- Something you are eating
- A task you are completing

Now go over this in your mind in a particular way
- Close your eyes
- Put your attention on it
- What does it mean?
- Notice how it looks
- Tastes?
- Smells?
- Feels?

Now discuss "on purpose"
- What is your purpose?
- What is your focus?
- Give it all of your attention

Be present in the moment
- Dismiss thoughts about the future
- Allow thoughts about the past to pass through and not stick
- As thoughts wander, bring yourself back to the present

Non-judgmentally
- Accept reality for what it is
- Just notice
- Cast judgments aside
- Detach from critical thoughts

Reflect on your experience:

_____

_____

Copyright 2016 © Jeff Riggenbach, *The Borderline Personality Disorder Toolbox*. All rights reserved.

Improving the Moment

This tool helps makes undesirable moments at least slightly better. Is there one positive aspect of what you are going through? Do you at least have someone helpful to go through the undesirable moments with you? If there is nothing desirable about this situation, can you focus on another aspect of your life that is better?

The next time you catch yourself saying, "I can't stand this anymore," **what are some general things you will consider doing that can make the moment slightly better?**

1. _____
   _____
   _____

2. _____
   _____
   _____

3. _____
   _____
   _____

Copyright 2016 © Jeff Riggenbach, *The Borderline Personality Disorder Toolbox*. All rights reserved.

IMAGERY

Our minds are more powerful than we realize. Consider how upset you can get when "flashing back" to an uncomfortable image. Or have you caught yourself saying, "I don't want to think about that now. . . I'll think about it later"? Many people avoid thinking about certain things because of the emotion they will feel if they "let themselves go there."

Similarly, we can harness that power by utilizing positive imagery. **Many people have a *safe place image:* a place they can go in their mind and find complete serenity, safety, or calm.** For many people, this is a sunny beach, a grassy meadow, or some place of that nature. For one of my patients who had experienced very little safety in her entire life, her "safe place" was the waiting room at our clinic.

Close your eyes. Let your mind convince your body you are there in this moment. Write out a description of your safe place image. Draw a picture if you like. This can be a useful tool during times of emotional turbulence.

_____

_____

_____

_____

_____

_____

Copyright 2016 © Jeff Riggenbach, *The Borderline Personality Disorder Toolbox*. All rights reserved.

MAKING MEANING IN YOUR LIFE

Victor Frankl was one of the very few in his group who survived a Nazi concentration camp. The experience, as horrific as it was, inspired his best-selling book *Man's Search for Meaning*. In it, he writes, "Life is never made unbearable by circumstances, but only by lack of meaning and purpose." Marty Antony has a technique he uses when working with people who have endured traumatic events which he calls the "silver lining technique."

Ask yourself the questions, **"What meaning can I make of this horrible experience?"** Even though it was inherently awful, is there some unique opportunity I am now 'qualified' for as a result of this experience that I was previously unqualified for? I have a patient who was shot in the head by police officers while attempting to steal a trooper's car as he was caught in a drug bust. He survived, but has lived the last 15 years of his life without eyes. After living a life of criminality for 7 years and spending the next 10 in prison, he now shares his testimony as part of a prison ministry.

Describe how you could use meaning in your life.

_____

_____

_____

_____

_____

_____

Copyright 2016 © Jeff Riggenbach, *The Borderline Personality Disorder Toolbox*. All rights reserved.

PRAYER TO HELP COPE

Prayer can be a powerful way to change our internal state. In a large scale study of schizophrenic patients, prayer was endorsed as one of the **most effective coping skills** for dealing with emotional distress brought about by psychotic symptoms. Few people reading this book will probably deal with psychotic symptoms, but most (if not all) deal with significant emotional distress. Seek to connect to God or a higher power in some way.

Write out a personal prayer that has meaning to you. If you are not at a place in your spiritual life to write out a personal prayer, use the Serenity Prayer.

_____

_____

_____

_____

_____

_____

Copyright 2016 © Jeff Riggenbach, *The Borderline Personality Disorder Toolbox*. All rights reserved.

RELAXATION TECHNIQUES

Many people with BPD suffer through a life of chaos. There are many different ways to relax. This one is not rocket science. **Guided imagery, deep breathing exercises, and progressive muscle relaxation are all ways to facilitate relaxation.** Wear comfortable clothing. Watch something mindless. Listen to relaxing music. Spend time with friends who help you relax. Engage in artwork or something creative.

Different things are relaxing to different people. Describe how you can use relaxation to calm yourself.

_____

_____

_____

_____

_____

_____

_____

Copyright 2016 © Jeff Riggenbach, *The Borderline Personality Disorder Toolbox*. All rights reserved.

One Thing In The Moment

People with BPD often experience racing thoughts. Racing thoughts contribute to intense emotions and it is easy to get overwhelmed. SLOW DOWN. Prioritize. Ask yourself: "Of all the thoughts swirling in my mind at this moment, what is the most important?" "What is the smallest step I could take in this moment?" Here's a tip: **No step is too small.** It is common for people NOT to choose helpful steps in the heat of the moment because whatever comes to mind seems too small. But remember, one small step each day and in a year you've made 365 steps and are likely at a different place in your life.

Describe how you could take "one thing at a time."

_____

_____

_____

_____

_____

_____

_____

Copyright 2016 © Jeff Riggenbach, *The Borderline Personality Disorder Toolbox*. All rights reserved.

Take a Vacation

Taking an actual vacation during times of distress is usually not possible. For some people, vacations are rare treats. Even if you can't go on an annual cruise, try to plan small getaways, if possible. Take a weekend away with a spouse or other enjoyable person. Spend a night at a local hotel. Just getting away for an evening out with your guy/girl friends can be a very helpful vacation of sorts. Take a day off work. These can keep our batteries charged.

"Vacations," in this context, can even mean shorter "get-aways." Step outside. Get a breath of fresh air. Watch an hour of reality TV. Call an old friend and talk about old times. Listen to your favorite music. Go for a drive. Some people even need to take a brief vacation from therapy and focus elsewhere for a while.

Describe how you could use "vacation time."

_____

_____

_____

_____

_____

_____

_____

Copyright 2016 © Jeff Riggenbach, *The Borderline Personality Disorder Toolbox*. All rights reserved.

ENCOURAGEMENT SCRIPT

The irony is that many people with BPD are great encouragers of others. Many have had someone in their life (or more than one) who was very critical. Often times, that critical voice gets internalized and that inner-critic now resides in us and can be our worst enemy.

Life can be hard. **But remind yourself you have survived a lot in life;** you probably have the resilience to survive this. Pretend you had a friend who was in a bad place; what would you say to them? Try to encourage yourself in the way you would someone else.

Write a script you could use to encourage yourself at times you get down or feel hopeless.

_____

_____

_____

_____

_____

_____

_____

_____

_____

Copyright 2016 © Jeff Riggenbach, *The Borderline Personality Disorder Toolbox*. All rights reserved.

DISTRACTION TECHNIQUES

A distraction technique might be defined as *any coping skill that requires thought*. For instance, taking a hot bath may be a good coping skill, but does it inherently require thought? A question to ask is: Can I still do this behavior and continuously stew on my upsetting thoughts? In the case of a bath, *yes*, it is possible to stare at the tiles in front of you and obsess over whatever has you worked up. So technically, a bath would not fit this definition of distraction.

On the other hand, writing a letter to someone requires you to think about what you are writing. Since we can't think two thoughts at the same time, there are at least periods we are focused off of the upsetting topic. Sometimes, you may have intrusive thoughts "jumping back" in your mind, but if that is the case, you can get at least temporary relief. It is also possible that the topic of your distraction will "take over" for a while and you may not think of the distressing event again for some period of time.

It should be noted that distraction can be unhealthy if it feeds your avoiding an event or topic you need to confront. Distraction techniques are only healthy when used as *temporary* measures to decrease the intensity of your mood so that you can be calmer and in a more rational place to confront events that need to be dealt with and for you to process them so they no longer affect you negatively.

List some distraction techniques that come to mind off the top of your head that you might try.

1. _____

   _____

2. _____

   _____

3. _____

   _____

4. _____

   _____

5. _____

   _____

Copyright 2016 © Jeff Riggenbach, *The Borderline Personality Disorder Toolbox*. All rights reserved.

Activities

Some people don't think of everyday activities we do as coping skills. However, it is true that some of the things we do naturally throughout our day can be done *purposefully* at certain times for specific purposes. Routine household tasks (even if they aren't fun!) **can be used to take our mind elsewhere.** Consider the following activities list.

- Read a book
- Call a friend
- Play a board game
- Go for a walk
- Take inventory in a cabinet
- Check out local garage sales
- Write in your journal
- Go dancing
- Look at magazines
- Cook something that requires a recipe
- Play computer games
- Take a donation to a local ministry or charity
- Play checkers
- Play chess
- Watch a TV show (actually follow the plot)
- Go geocaching
- Garden
- Read a magazine
- Go window shopping
- Text a friend
- Crochet
- Knit
- Do beadwork
- Count coins
- Sing

- Invite people over
- Go to a park
- Paint
- Do yoga
- Play fantasy football
- Watch a funny movie
- Go to a lake
- Play on a smart phone
- Go through old CDs
- Color
- Email a friend
- Have responsible sex
- Try to juggle
- Clean out a closet
- Volunteer
- Write a thank you note
- Scrapbook
- Meditate
- Play the piano
- Surf the internet
- Say a prayer
- Go to the library
- Read the Bible
- Go to an AA meeting
- Plan a trip

List some activities you could try the next time you are experiencing intense emotions.

1._____

2._____

3._____

4._____

5._____

6. _____

7. _____

8. _____

9. _____

10. _____

Copyright 2016 © Jeff Riggenbach, *The Borderline Personality Disorder Toolbox*. All rights reserved.

Contribute To Others

It is well established that "getting outside ourselves" can often be a helpful ingredient for treating depression. **Making a contribution to the well-being of someone else can be a useful distraction and a powerful way to improve one's mood.** Buy a $5 gift. Listen to someone else's problems. Volunteer for a local cause or charity. List several ways you will consider contributing.

1. _____

_____

2. _____

_____

3. _____

_____

4. _____

_____

5. _____

_____

Copyright 2016 © Jeff Riggenbach, *The Borderline Personality Disorder Toolbox*. All rights reserved.

Compare & Reevaluate Your Perspective

You may have heard a mental health professional tell you, "Stop comparing yourself to others.... it doesn't help!" The reality is that we all make comparisons. It only becomes a problem for people with perfectionistic thinking who are constantly evaluating themselves unfairly, typically by comparing themselves to someone "above them" in a particular area, thus reinforcing "what a failure they are." If you are "below" someone in a certain area, acknowledge that. But also recognize you are "above" many others in that exact same area. Most people don't compare themselves with those individuals (unless you are a narcissist!). It would then only be fair to yourself to acknowledge that you are "better" than others in certain areas as well.

We all have strengths and weaknesses in different areas and that is OK. The reality is there are only a few elite people in any given area and only a few "bottom dwellers." The rest of us are all somewhere in between. So rather than compare yourself with a model who is 20 years younger than you, how about comparing yourself to someone about your age who has the same work and family obligations as you do? That would be fairer, don't you think?

Sometimes, I am not feeling the best when I am on the road giving seminars or conferences. But I always remind myself of the time I was in Honolulu one night receiving IV fluids and giving a lecture a few hours later. Recalling that event, can honestly tell myself, "I got through that; I can undoubtedly get through this."

Comparison can be a powerful way of reevaluating perspective. Use the following space to describe how you can use the skill of comparison.

_____

_____

_____

_____

_____

_____

Copyright 2016 © Jeff Riggenbach, *The Borderline Personality Disorder Toolbox*. All rights reserved.

CHANGE EMOTIONS

Many people with BPD feel so intensely miserable, they may often look for a "quick feel good." That is, they may search for something external to do to themselves to change their internal feelings. Often, these are unhealthy behaviors and lead to worse long-term consequences. But individuals can substitute healthy behaviors that serve the same function and have fewer damaging consequences. Watching a funny or touching movie, painting fingernails and toenails, and listening to emotional moving lyrics are all ways to change emotions. I have one patient who has four specific "go to" songs that, due to their meaning to her, will work every time.

Here's a tip: Many listen to depressing music when they are depressed. This can have a validating effect if only done for short period of time. But be sure not to get stuck there. The 90s grunge band *Nirvana* was an example of a group who struck a chord with their generational angst. . . and their lead singer, Kurt Cobain, eventually committed suicide. Listening to music of this nature can be helpful for a very brief period of time. Otherwise, I warn my patients not to get stuck in "Nirvana fan syndrome."

Others are able to use touching or humorous imagery, have responsible sex, or focus on gratitude. **List several things you could try that might help change your emotions in the future.**

1. _____

_____

2. _____

_____

3. _____

_____

4. _____

_____

5. _____

_____

Copyright 2016 © Jeff Riggenbach, *The Borderline Personality Disorder Toolbox*. All rights reserved.

Push Away Worries

Pushing away refers to putting one's problem in a box, locking it in the closet for a while, and choosing to go deal with it later. In his best-selling book *The Worry Cure*, Bob Leahy describes "worry time." He suggests that, when a worrisome thought comes, you write it down, put it in your "worry tub" (whatever that may be), and set it aside until your designated "worry time." **Assign a time each day (perhaps 30 minutes) during which you will worry about your problems.** Outside of that 30 minutes, push away unwelcomed concerns that invite themselves into your head.

In the space provided, describe how you could use the tool of "pushing away."

_____

_____

_____

_____

_____

_____

Copyright 2016 © Jeff Riggenbach, *The Borderline Personality Disorder Toolbox*. All rights reserved.

Positive Thoughts

Many people are generally unaware of many of their thoughts. So the first step in changing thoughts is **becoming aware of and recognizing the thoughts we are actually having**. In the space below list some positive or healthy thoughts you might be able to use next time your thoughts are not serving you well.

1. _____
   _____
   _____

2. _____
   _____
   _____

3. _____
   _____
   _____

4. _____
   _____
   _____

5. _____
   _____
   _____

Copyright 2016 © Jeff Riggenbach, *The Borderline Personality Disorder Toolbox*. All rights reserved.

Sensations to regulate emotions

Many people with BPD find that sensations can often help modulate intense emotions. Use the following tool to help you evaluate methods of using the five senses to assist in regulating your emotions.

Hearing: (i.e., music, relaxation CDs, running water, birds chirping, etc.)

The following sounds can be soothing to me: _____

_____

_____

Sight: (i.e., paintings, other artwork, calming scenes, clouds, other nature, etc.)

The following things I can see can be soothing to me: _____

_____

_____

Smell: (i.e., incense, candles, aromatherapy, pine trees, fabric softener, etc.)

The following smells can be soothing for me: _____

_____

_____

Taste: (i.e., chocolate, raisins, ice cream, chewing gum, candy or lasagna)

The following tastes can be soothing to me: _____

_____

_____

Touch: (i.e., stuffed animals, comfy PJs, freshly washed sheets, massage, etc.)

The following things I can touch can be soothing to me: _____

_____

_____

Copyright 2016 © Jeff Riggenbach, *The Borderline Personality Disorder Toolbox*. All rights reserved.

Soothing Strategies

Many individuals with BPD were not soothed as children. Some were severely abused or neglected, and others were just parented by mothers who were not overly nurturing. Also, some people are born with a predisposition to be more sensitive than others. When needs are not met or feelings get hurt, it is important to have a set of coping skills that can help de-escalate us.

If you have a friend who has a calming effect on you, connecting to that person is often a preferable way to alleviate intense emotions. However, often people are not available when we need them. So it is also important to have some ways to self-soothe. **A soothing strategy might be defined as any coping skill that has a *calming* effect or helps one to relax in some way.** Commonly-used soothing strategies include taking a bubble bath, getting a massage, listening to calming music, applying lotion, watching a sunset, enjoying nature, snuggling with a pet.

Soothing strategies I might use include:

_____

_____

_____

_____

_____

Copyright 2016 © Jeff Riggenbach, *The Borderline Personality Disorder Toolbox*. All rights reserved.

OPPOSITE ACTION

There was an episode of *Seinfeld* where George stated, "Everything I do is wrong!" So he decided that any time he had a decision to make he would think about what he would normally do and just *do the exact opposite*. This became known in Seinfeld circles as "the opposite George" episode. While its extreme form portrayed in the episode was actually quite humorous, a version of this concept can be helpful in emotion regulation.

In my previous book *The CBT Toolbox*, I describe "go-to" behaviors: Those are behaviors that many of us get into a rut of performing in response to certain "autopilot" thoughts and the emotions that accompany them. While different people have different specific "go-to" behaviors, many themes can be identified that are common when feeling specific emotions.

For instance, when people are feeling anxious or fearful, they tend to avoid. When people feel depressed, they often become inactive. When people are angry, they often lash out at others. **The problem is that the very behaviors we feel like doing, if we give in to our autopilot thoughts and emotions, are the very behaviors that reinforce our unhealthy mindsets and keep us stuck.** So acting in the opposite manner of these urges is actually the key to getting "unstuck." The table below summarizes emotions frequently experienced and "go-to" behaviors associated with them, and opposite action alternatives.

Emotion	"Go-To" Urge	Opposite Action
Anxiety/Fear	Shut down, withdraw, avoid, get quiet	Face fears, be assertive, confront situations
Depression	Isolate, be inactive, focus on negative, overeat, under-eat	Engage socially, express feelings, exercise, practice gratitude, balanced meals
Anger (toward others)	Lash out, yell, use profanity, threaten	Count to 10, talk kindly, compliment
Self-Hate/Shame	Put self down, self-harm, sabotaging behaviors	Treat self well, self-compassion, self-affirmations

Use the following table to pinpoint your "go-to" behaviors when you feel a certain way and then identify some "opposite actions" you may be willing to try.

Copyright 2016 © Jeff Riggenbach, *The Borderline Personality Disorder Toolbox*. All rights reserved.

OPPOSITE ACTION

Emotion	"Go-To" Urge	Opposite Action

Copyright 2016 © Jeff Riggenbach, *The Borderline Personality Disorder Toolbox*. All rights reserved.

PLEASURABLE EVENTS

When we don't feel good, we don't feel like doing anything. This is one of the tough ironies about depression in particular. The very thing that we need to do to get better is the exact thing we do not *FEEL* like doing. The reality is that **doing something usually makes us feel better**. When dealing with unpleasant intense moods, it can be meaningful to pick something that can give us pleasure. Before you list your possible pleasurable events, consider the following as possibilities.

- Go to a movie
- Sunbathe
- Watch something funny on TV
- Spend time with someone who makes you laugh
- Play a board game
- Play a game on your smart phone
- Listen to music
- Write about an old positive memory
- Plan a trip
- Remember beautiful scenery
- Color
- Rearrange your house
- Responsible sex
- Knit, crochet, or something else artistic
- Do something spontaneous

Describe some pleasurable activities you can use:

1. _____

2. _____

3. _____

4. _____

5. _____

Copyright 2016 © Jeff Riggenbach, *The Borderline Personality Disorder Toolbox*. All rights reserved.

MASTERY OF A "TO-DO" LIST

Some people feel especially good about themselves when they are able to accomplish things. Productivity can enhance mood. Get good at a particular skill. Make a "to-do" list. As you accomplish each thing on the list, cross it off, give yourself credit for what you did, and move on to the next item.

It's important to make your to-do lists reasonable, so you are likely to get them done. Some people get too ambitious and make lists too long, do not accomplish them, and this exercise actually backfires and people feel worse.

Begin with short lists and go from there. As you complete an item, add another as you go along. Consider how you may use mastery exercises to feel accomplished. A few examples might include:

- Get out of bed
- Brush my teeth
- Take a shower
- Put on make-up
- Eat breakfast
- Clean a room in the house
- Run needed errands
- Make medical appointments
- Complete a project for work or school
- Open / sort mail
- Pay bills
- Feed the dog
- Do one load of laundry
- Complete a project in the garage
- Get oil change
- Work at a hobby

Describe some tasks that might help you feel accomplished:

1. _____

2. _____

3. _____

4. _____

5. _____

Copyright 2016 © Jeff Riggenbach, *The Borderline Personality Disorder Toolbox*. All rights reserved.

OBJECTIVE EFFECTIVENESS

It is often difficult for people with BPD to be assertive. Many find themselves being the "mouse" that always gets run over and never gets their needs met. Others become "the bitch" who goes off on people "because they deserved it" with no regard for others' feelings or experience and no regard for what is in their best interest in the big picture.

Interpersonal effectiveness skills help people attempt to 1) get what they want/need, 2) get what they want/need in a way that maintains the relationship and 3) get what they want/need in a way that maintains the relationship and also maintains their self-respect. The first part of this is called *Objective Effectiveness*. **This principal is intended to help keep people focused on the objective at hand, or what you really want.** This is important because, during conflict, people with BPD often get caught up in other motivations, such as not being criticized or getting someone back. When considering how to be effective in meeting your objective, consider asking yourself the following questions:

1. **What is my objective here? (i.e., what is it that I really want?)**

2. **What things have I tried in similar situations in the past that have not worked or backfired that I want to avoid this time?**

3. **What is the best way to go about trying to get what I want?**

Copyright 2016 © Jeff Riggenbach, *The Borderline Personality Disorder Toolbox*. All rights reserved.

Describing Behavior

When emotions get intense, it is easy for many people to become demeaning, judgmental or engage in name calling. While devaluing someone, or seeing them as "all bad," these statements may *seem* accurate and might *feel good in the moment*, but this thinking and behavior will only make things worse in the long run. *Describing* a behavior is better understood by some with the help of detective Joe Friday from TV classic *Dragnet* and the catchphrase attributed to him: "just the facts, ma'am." **Describing is only observing behavior and describing it.** It does not involve labeling, judging, or evaluating. The better we can get at describing vs. labeling and name-calling, the better we get at regulating intense emotions. The differences are illustrated with the following statements made by one of my patients.

Judging/Labeling statement: "Dad is an uncaring, dishonest chauvinist who hates me."

Describing Statement(s): "Dad said 'no' when I asked him to help me with my medical bills. I think he might have the money, but he is choosing not to give it to me. He has called women names in the past."

Try to notice yourself 3 times this week having judging or labeling thoughts or making comments, and use the table below to practice only describing the events rather than labeling or evaluating.

Situation	Labeling Thought/Comment	Describe ("Just the Facts")

 Copyright 2016 © Jeff Riggenbach, *The Borderline Personality Disorder Toolbox*. All rights reserved.

Express

After describing a situation or a behavior, then is the time to express emotions. It is important to let others know how we feel, but in an appropriate way. One commonly used and helpful way to express feelings involves the use of "I" statements. **"I" statements often keep others from feeling attacked and increase the chances you will be heard and actually get what you want.**

"When you have the money and choose not to help me when I need it, I sometimes feel like you don't care about me," is a lot more effective than "I hate you - you are a selfish and stingy rich man!"

Use the blanks below to log some situations that are upsetting to you and thoughts about how you could express yourself appropriately.

Situation:

_____

_____

Appropriate Expression:

_____

_____

Situation:

_____

_____

Appropriate Expression:

_____

_____

Situation:

_____

_____

Appropriate Expression:

_____

_____

Copyright 2016 © Jeff Riggenbach, *The Borderline Personality Disorder Toolbox*. All rights reserved.

Assert/Ask For What You Want

Many people with BPD grew up in families where it was not OK to ask for what you wanted, state your opinion or get your needs met. Maybe it was "selfish" to even have needs. A tough lesson you will learn, hopefully, during your course of treatment for BPD is that all human beings have needs. And that it is **OK to have needs and to ask for them to be met**. Identify what your needs are in a relationship. Ask clearly for what you want or need. Some find it helpful to use the "I think, I feel, I want" format.

I think ... Describe the facts around a situation that was hurtful. Make every attempt not to be judging or blaming.

> [blank box]

I feel ... Describe a feeling you had in a recent hurtful interaction.

> [blank box]

I want ... Ask for what you want in the relationship.

> [blank box]

Also, sometimes assertive communication involves saying no to requests others make of us. Just because somebody asks doesn't mean we have to say yes. And, if someone puts you "on the spot" and you are not sure, it is almost always OK to say, "I need to think about it and get back with you." This gives you time to think through a decision and not say "yes" when it is really in your best interest to say "no."

People/Requests in my life I need to say "no" to include:

_____

_____

_____

Copyright 2016 © Jeff Riggenbach, *The Borderline Personality Disorder Toolbox*. All rights reserved.

Reward/Reinforce

Let others know what is in it for them. How will getting what you want benefit them? What will they get out of it? Will they save money by giving you what you want? Will they get to act in accordance with one of their values? **Will one of their causes benefit? It can help to think of people in your life with wants or needs and identify ways of rewarding them for helping you.**

Person	Reward/What they Value

Copyright 2016 © Jeff Riggenbach, *The Borderline Personality Disorder Toolbox*. All rights reserved.

Mindfully Stay Focused

One technique for staying mindfully focused when asking for something is the "broken record technique." **This is where you continue to state/ask for the same thing regardless of where the other person tries to take the conversation.** Some people may get annoyed you are saying the same thing over and over again. Some will just try to get you off focus. Some may be so emotional themselves that they don't even realize you are doing it the first several times. Sometimes it is necessary to modify our volume level or tone of voice to get the response we want, but staying focused is important in any conversation.

Some examples include:

- Stay focused
- Remember my goals
- If I lose my cool, she wins

Some phrases I could use to stay mindfully focused are:

1. _____

2. _____

3. _____

4. _____

5. _____

Copyright 2016 © Jeff Riggenbach, *The Borderline Personality Disorder Toolbox*. All rights reserved.

APPEAR CONFIDENT

Twelve step programs use the phrase, "fake it till you make it." In general, this is usually bad advice. However, when having difficult conversations that bring out insecurities, it can be helpful to practice this technique. **Act as if you feel confident even if you do not.**

Use an assertive tone of voice, make eye contact, and use confident body language. Picture yourself as someone you know in your life who is confident. Listen to music that bolsters your confidence prior to having the conversation. Do something that, even if temporary, will help you portray an aura of confidence. It is believed that dogs can "smell fear" in people. Oftentimes people can tell when others are scared, as well, and some will take advantage of that.

Some examples include:

- Dress like a supervisor even though I am not one yet

- While talking to my boss, pretend she is my little sister who I can be assertive with

- Remind yourself of the song lyric "If you don't fight for you, nobody will"

My strategies for appearing confident are:

1. _____

2. _____

3. _____

4. _____

5. _____

Copyright 2016 © Jeff Riggenbach, *The Borderline Personality Disorder Toolbox*. All rights reserved.

NECESSARY NEGOTIATION

If you ask for something and the other person disagrees, some negotiation may be necessary. Negotiation is often very difficult for individuals with BPD. Many think versions of, "if I don't get exactly what I want, I don't want anything from them." This way of thinking ("black and white" thinking is addressed in later chapters) often leads to people getting NOTHING they want when, if they were able to negotiate, they may at least get SOME of what they want. Marsha Linehan recommends using the **VASE acronym as a guide for negotiating**.

Validate that you see where the other person is coming from. Then tell them where you are coming from.

Ask the other person for a compromise. Is there a way for both of you to get part of what you want?

Suggest alternatives. Are there other ways to approach the disagreement? What are you willing to give up? What is it necessary for you to keep? Some people think giving in is "losing" if they don't get everything they want. But remember, getting part of what you want is better than getting none of what you want!

Express yourself in a kind voice. An angry tone or aggressive manner is unlikely to get you what you want.

Some examples include:

Remember: Getting part of what I want is better than getting none of what I want.

V̲alidate: I understand your need to be careful with the budget you are responsible for.

A̲sk for compromise: I will agree to accept the minimum raise at this time if you will agree to review me again in 6 months when you have a new budget rather than the typical one year.

S̲uggest alternatives: If the current budget keeps you from giving me the raise we both believe I deserve, how about giving me some extra paid time off this quarter?

E̲xpress yourself in a kind voice. Say the above kindly. Pay attention to your wording. Monitor your tone of voice.

Copyright 2016 © Jeff Riggenbach, *The Borderline Personality Disorder Toolbox*. All rights reserved.

My strategies for negotiation

V_____

A_____

S_____

E_____

Copyright 2016 © Jeff Riggenbach, *The Borderline Personality Disorder Toolbox*. All rights reserved.

RELATIONAL EFFECTIVENESS

Relational effectiveness has to do with achieving our objective in a way that keeps the relationship intact. Often, our most intense conflicts are with those whom we really care about the most. This sounds strange to some people, but it is only the people who we care about who usually have the power to get us that angry. Rarely does a checker in the grocery store have the ability to produce feelings of rage in us.

Many people with BPD know how to get their way, but often do so in a way that alienates those around them. While in the heat of the moment, many individuals with BPD will say, "I don't care," yet when they find themselves alone in their apartment, the reality is they hate being alone so much they actually care a great deal. Questions often helpful to ask to maintain relationship effectiveness are:

1. **How do I want this person to feel about me tomorrow?**

2. **How do I want this person to feel about me a week from now?**

3. **Will I need this person in any way in the future?**

4. **What are some things I have done in similar situations in the past that have backfired and damaged relationships I wish I still had?**

5. **What is the best way to handle this situation that will likely maintain the relationship?**

Copyright 2016 © Jeff Riggenbach, *The Borderline Personality Disorder Toolbox*. All rights reserved.

DEVELOPING A GENTLE TONE

Being gentle is difficult for many with BPD, as many get easily agitated and come across in ways they do not mean to. **Remaining gentle requires a mindful awareness of tone of voice and how one is coming across.** Some even record conversations with people. Many are astounded how they came across when they go back and watch the video of the conversation. Practice in front of a mirror. Practice with a friend. Get better at observing your tone and bringing it down even when you feel your emotions escalating. Developing a gentle tone takes self-awareness and practice.

Some examples include:

- Practice in my support group

- Practice with my therapist

- Ask someone else who was present for one of my exchanges how they perceived me as coming across

Describe some ways you could work on developing a gentle tone of voice.

1. _____

2. _____

3. _____

4. _____

5. _____

Copyright 2016 © Jeff Riggenbach, *The Borderline Personality Disorder Toolbox*. All rights reserved.

Be Interested In Where
Others Are Coming From

It is easy for people with BPD to be so concerned with not getting taken advantage of again that they are not tuned into the other person. Convey an interest in them as a person. **Try to see where they are coming from and be interested in their point of view.** Try to see things the way they do. Try to feel what they feel. Even if you don't agree with them on these specifics, you know what if feels like to feel frustrated. Be interested in where they are coming from.

Describe some ways you can convey interest in someone else's point of view:

_____

_____

_____

_____

Copyright 2016 © Jeff Riggenbach, *The Borderline Personality Disorder Toolbox*. All rights reserved.

Validate

Think of how important it is for you to feel validated. How much more likely are you to cooperate with what someone else wants if you feel understood? Likewise, when asking someone else for something, it is important that we help them feel understood. **You can validate their emotions even if you don't agree with everything they are saying.** The more they feel understood, the more likely they will be to give you what you want and the relationship will stay cordial.

Some examples include:

- I know what it is like to be out of your element
- I know what is like to be angry
- I know what it is like to have a difficult past
- I know what it is like to be unhappy

Describe some ways you might validate others:

1. _____

2. _____

3. _____

4. _____

5. _____

Copyright 2016 © Jeff Riggenbach, *The Borderline Personality Disorder Toolbox*. All rights reserved.

Easy Manner

An easy manner involves treating others with kindness. Try to stay relaxed. The more "worked up" you get, the more others will feel the need to put their guard up. **The nicer we are to others, the more likely it is they will be nice to us in return.**

Some examples include:

- Practice being more laid back

- Recognize when emotions are intense, and knowing it's not a time to act

- Use deep breathing or music to keep me calm

Describe ways you can work on developing an easy manner.

_____

_____

_____

Copyright 2016 © Jeff Riggenbach, *The Borderline Personality Disorder Toolbox*. All rights reserved.

SELF-RESPECT EFFECTIVENESS

Self-respect effectiveness has to do with trying to get what you want or need in a way that leaves you feeling good about yourself afterwards. Many people with BPD get what they want and some even get what they want while maintaining relationships, but do so by acting in such a way that makes them hate themselves afterwards. If, on your way to getting what you want, you have to act in ways that you will later be ashamed of, it is almost never worth it. **The most important thing is to maintain your integrity so you can feel good about yourself with the choices you made.**

1. **How will I feel about myself tomorrow if I say/do _____?**

2. **When I've hated myself in the past, what are some things I have done in response?**

3. **What can I do in this situation that will cause me to feel good about myself tomorrow?**

> Remember:
> - All I can control is me
> - I don't want to hate myself when this is over
> - The most important thing is to be consistent with my values so I can be proud of me, regardless of what he does

Copyright 2016 © Jeff Riggenbach, *The Borderline Personality Disorder Toolbox*. All rights reserved.

Fair and Respectful Negotiations

Remain fair in your negotiations. Do not use demeaning words or put downs. **Treat others with respect and if you are tempted to fight "unfair" catch yourself.** Take a break if you need to. In your anger, do not allow yourself to use tactics that are "below the belt," even though in that moment you do not care. Remind yourself that you will care later. You might feel justified in the moment, but this will not help you respect yourself in the long term.

List some things that you think may be important for you to remember to "fight fair."

1. _____

2. _____

3. _____

4. _____

5. _____

Copyright 2016 © Jeff Riggenbach, *The Borderline Personality Disorder Toolbox*. All rights reserved.

No Apologies

Do NOT apologize for standing up for what you believe in. While it IS healthy to apologize when we do something wrong, **it is NOT healthy to apologize when we did NOT do anything wrong**. Some people grew up in families where a parent was frequently yelling or being critical, so the child believed they were always in the wrong. Many internalize these messages and carry them into adulthood. Thus, they often feel guilty just because someone is upset.

Saying, "I'm sorry," when you really didn't do anything wrong continues to reinforce those unhealthy beliefs about yourself and makes you sicker. Don't apologize for standing up for your values.

List some situations or relationships in your life that tend to influence you to apologize even when it is not good for you to do so:

1. _____

   _____

2. _____

   _____

3. _____

   _____

4. _____

   _____

5. _____

   _____

Copyright 2016 © Jeff Riggenbach, *The Borderline Personality Disorder Toolbox*. All rights reserved.

Stick To Your Values

Identify what some of your values are and ways that you can stand up for them. Some areas to consider include:

- Religious/Spiritual beliefs
- Love
- Forgiveness
- Family
- Intimate relationships
- Friendships
- Financial success

- Self-esteem
- Personal growth
- Physical beauty or attractiveness
- Health
- Kindness
- Learning
- Fun

Some of my values include:

_____

_____

_____

_____

_____

Copyright 2016 © Jeff Riggenbach, *The Borderline Personality Disorder Toolbox*. All rights reserved.

Be Truthful

Be honest with yourself and others. Attempting to manipulate or deceive others is not a good way to keep friends or to feel good about yourself. Take responsibility and be as honest as you can be. This will only help you respect yourself in the long run.

Some areas in which I can work on being truthful include:

1. _____

_____

2. _____

_____

3. _____

_____

4. _____

_____

5. _____

_____

Copyright 2016 © Jeff Riggenbach, *The Borderline Personality Disorder Toolbox*. All rights reserved.

DIARY CARD SAMPLE

Diary cards can be a powerful tool for monitoring your own recovery on a day-to-day basis. It asks for a date (for some people with BPD who struggle with regular dissociation, there is benefit in simply writing the date down every day), mood ranges (highest and lowest any given day, because as mentioned in the mood swings sections, moods can change multiple times in one day), whether or not a target behavior was engaged in, and prompts for skills used in different areas.

Date: _8-15_

Depression _2_ to _8_

Anxiety _5_ to _9_

Anger _2_ to _5_

Suicidal ideation: N (Y)   Active (Passive)

Destructive Behaviors I engaged in today: Binged, lashed out

Skills Used: Distraction, mindfulness, challenging thoughts, exercise

Soothing: None

Distraction: Tried watching you tube videos

Opposite Action: Anxious & tried to face fear

Mindfulness or Challenging: 5 min practice focus on breath

Interpersonal Effectiveness: None

Positive Steps I took today: Reached out when I needed to, resisted urge to cut. completed homework. did not fight with mom when she baited me

Copyright 2016 © Jeff Riggenbach, *The Borderline Personality Disorder Toolbox*. All rights reserved.

Diary Card

Date: _____   Depression _____ to _____

Anxiety _____ to _____

Anger _____ to _____

Suicidal ideation: N   Y   Active Passive

Destructive behaviors I engaged in today: _____

_____

Skills Used: _____

Soothing: _____

Distraction: _____

Opposite Action: _____

Mindfulness or Challenging: _____

Interpersonal Effectiveness: _____

Positive Steps I took today: _____

_____

_____

Copyright 2016 © Jeff Riggenbach, *The Borderline Personality Disorder Toolbox*. All rights reserved.

CHAPTER 6

CBT Tools

Cognitive Behavior Therapy (CBT) is the most empirically supported form of treatment for most mental health related issues. Just because some specialized strategies and tools are needed (such as Dialectical Behavior Therapy skills, Schema Focused Therapy, and crisis management skills) for BPD does not mean basic CBT skills cannot be helpful as well.

Technically (we try not to be too technical in this book) DBT and SFT skills are considered cognitive behavioral therapies. Traditional CBT skills are a foundational starting point for people with BPD.

FINDING MY BLIND SPOTS

The term "ego-syntonic" came from the Freudian concept of the "observing ego." Freud theorized that individuals with personality disorders lacked this observing ego, or the ability to distance themselves and objectively observe their own behavior. The reality is that every person has some "blind spots" in their personalities: parts of us that other people see in us better than we can see in ourselves.

Some people have difficulty seeing negative aspects of themselves (weaknesses) and others have difficulty accurately seeing positive aspects (strengths) in themselves. **Identifying these blind spots is essential for recovery from BPD.** Use the following tool to attempt to identify your blind spots. You may want to ask those who know you best and will shoot straight with you. Try hard not to be defensive. These can be hard to hear at first.

My Blind Spots

Some STRENGTHS others have said they see in me that I have hard time seeing are:

1. _____

2. _____

3. _____

Some WEAKNESSES other people have said they see in me that I have trouble seeing are:

1. _____

2. _____

3. _____

Some of my behaviors that others have verbalized concern about that I do not see as problems are:

1. _____

2. _____

3. _____

Copyright 2016 © Jeff Riggenbach, *The Borderline Personality Disorder Toolbox*. All rights reserved.

DEVELOPING INSIGHT

Perhaps you have heard the expression "Change = Insight + Action." We cannot change what we do not view as a problem (because we see no need to change). So developing insight into these blind spots is essential for recovery. **Sometimes insight can be developed by analyzing the behaviors that others are concerned with and evaluating them in terms of consequences or potential consequences**.

As hard as it is, try to keep an open mind. You will have that little voice inside your head saying, "but, this really isn't that bad because..." Don't let that stop you from developing this skill. We will have a tool for that later.

Example:

Behavior : _Broke into ex-girlfriend's house after she broke up with me_

    Historical/Possible Legal Consequence: _Get arrested, 2 nights in jail, probation_

    Historical/Possible Health Consequence: _None that I can think of_

    Historical/Possible Spiritual Consequence: _Guilt, shame - not the type of values I want to live my life by_

    Historical/Possible Financial Consequence: _Had to pay a fine_

    Historical/Possible Relational Consequence: _Lost any chance I had of getting her back, strained relationship with my parents when I asked them to bail me out_

Behavior : _____

    Historical/Possible Legal Consequence: _____

    Historical/Possible Health Consequence: _____

    Historical/Possible Spiritual Consequence: _____

    Historical/Possible Financial Consequence: _____

    Historical/Possible Relational Consequence: _____

Behavior : _____

    Historical/Possible Legal Consequence: _____

    Historical/Possible Health Consequence: _____

    Historical/Possible Spiritual Consequence: _____

    Historical/Possible Financial Consequence: _____

    Historical/Possible Relational Consequence: _____

How my destructive behaviors have or could hurt me:

_____

_____

Copyright 2016 © Jeff Riggenbach, *The Borderline Personality Disorder Toolbox*. All rights reserved.

	Destructive Behavior	**Results**
1.	_____	_____
	_____	_____
	_____	_____
2.	_____	_____
	_____	_____
	_____	_____
3.	_____	_____
	_____	_____
	_____	_____
4.	_____	_____
	_____	_____
	_____	_____
5.	_____	_____
	_____	_____
	_____	_____

My destructive behavior has hurt the following people in my life:

_____

_____

It has hurt them in the following ways:

_____

_____

Copyright 2016 © Jeff Riggenbach, *The Borderline Personality Disorder Toolbox*. All rights reserved.

Identify Target Behaviors

It is the rare person who wants to stay miserable. But many are resistant to give up the coping skills they have learned along the way that are keeping them miserable. All negative coping skills *work* in the short term, or we wouldn't use them.

So what makes them unhealthy? The DSM-5 that clinicians use to make diagnoses has a fancy term called *functional impairment*. Simply put, a *negative* coping skill has to *hurt* you in some way in the long term. **So any behavior that hurts your relationships, your finances, your legal status, your family life, your physical health, and/or your spiritual or emotional well-being, even if it makes you feel better in the short term is a manifestation of your BPD.**

Because some with BPD have difficulty with insight, it can be helpful to ask a friend or loved one what behaviors you are currently engaging in that they are concerned about. Even if you fail to see how it is harmful, a willingness to consider working on this may make a big difference in helping you minimize your strong emotions. Another way to identify behaviors to target may be to ask yourself, "When I feel emotions the strongest, what are some of my 'go to' behaviors to alleviate my distress?"

Due to the fact that everyone's BPD is different, target behaviors can vary drastically from person to person. Some common target behaviors include cutting, binge drinking, other impulsive drug use, spending episodes, impulsive sex, and episodes of rage. Others may just feel intense emotions but then just shut down or avoid. Still others may target specific behaviors within relationships (frequent break-ups, put-downs, the "silent treatment", etc.). Take a moment to identify some target behaviors you are willing to work on.

My Target Behaviors

1. _____

2. _____

3. _____

4. _____

5. _____

Copyright 2016 © Jeff Riggenbach, *The Borderline Personality Disorder Toolbox*. All rights reserved.

PROBLEM-SOLVING

What exactly are the problems you are facing? What is a problem to you often isn't a problem to others. What is a problem to others may not be a problem for you. Some problems are multifaceted, having several dimensions. That is, what may be seen as a single problem may really involve a series of problems: As people like to say, "It's complicated."

However, just because a situation is complicated doesn't mean it can't be resolved. Enlist friends, family, or a therapist to help you identify, specifically, what your problems are and then rank them in terms of importance (i.e., 1 = "must solve first," and 2, 3, 4, or 5, [depending on how many problems you have] = "can wait").

My Problem Log

1. _____

2. _____

3. _____

4. _____

5. _____

Once you have created your problem log and have decided which problem to start with, it is time to start generating options. It is often helpful to generate three to five options, or *things you could do.* This doesn't mean you will do those things; it just gives you a menu of options to choose from. People who struggle with black-and-white thinking often have difficulty even generating options.

For instance, one of my patients who was trying to solve the problem of deciding whether to spend Christmas at the home of a family member where she felt uncomfortable was asked in group to generate options. She said, "What do you mean, options? I don't have any!" The group then assured her that she did and challenged her to come up with five. "What do you mean five options?" she said, "I go, or I don't go." Her black-and-white thinking kept her from generating the middle-ground alternatives that the group was then able to help her develop, such as:

1. Not going at all

2. Going for just an hour

3. Going, but telling an aunt who would be there how uncomfortable she was and planning to "hang out mainly with her"

4. Going and staying as long as she could, but leaving as soon as her father started being critical

5. Having a friend "on call" to contact if things got bad

6. Taking a friend with her

7. Going and staying the whole time no matter what

Copyright 2016 © Jeff Riggenbach, *The Borderline Personality Disorder Toolbox*. All rights reserved.

This list of options the group helped her generate gave her several middle-ground alternatives to just "going or not going." Take a few minutes to consider what your options are. Remember to write them all down even if, at first thought, you do not think you will choose a particular option.

Five possible things I could do to solve the identified problem are:

1. _____

2. _____

3. _____

4. _____

5. _____

Now it is time to choose one option and see what happens! Consider these general tips first:

- When presented with a problem, always wait 30 minutes or longer, if possible, before making a decision. It is almost always acceptable to say, "I need to think about that for a while. When can I get back to you?"

- Never make a major life decision while in an episode. Chances are, you won't solve your problem and may make it worse.

- After thinking rationally, calming down, and processing with a member of your support team, make the decision you believe to be best for you.

Not all attempts to solve problems work. If a solution doesn't work, don't *"should"* yourself (beat yourself up). Try again. **Use the following log to help track your problems and your attempted solutions. Remember to use a different log for different problems, as some attempted solutions that may not work at all for one problem may work splendidly for another.**

Copyright 2016 © Jeff Riggenbach, *The Borderline Personality Disorder Toolbox*. All rights reserved.

PROBLEM-SOLVING LOG

Problem: _____

Date	Attempted Solution	Ways This Helped	Ways This Didn't Help	Worth Trying Again (Y/N)?

Copyright 2016 © Jeff Riggenbach, *The Borderline Personality Disorder Toolbox*. All rights reserved.

IDENTIFYING EMOTIONS

Some people with BPD are very good at expressing their feelings. Others have difficulty recognizing feelings, giving names to feelings, or even recognizing that they have feelings at all. The following "feelings face sheet" is often helpful for aiding people in identifying what feelings they are actually having. Using the face sheet tool, pick out several emotions that seem to describe best what feelings you commonly experience.

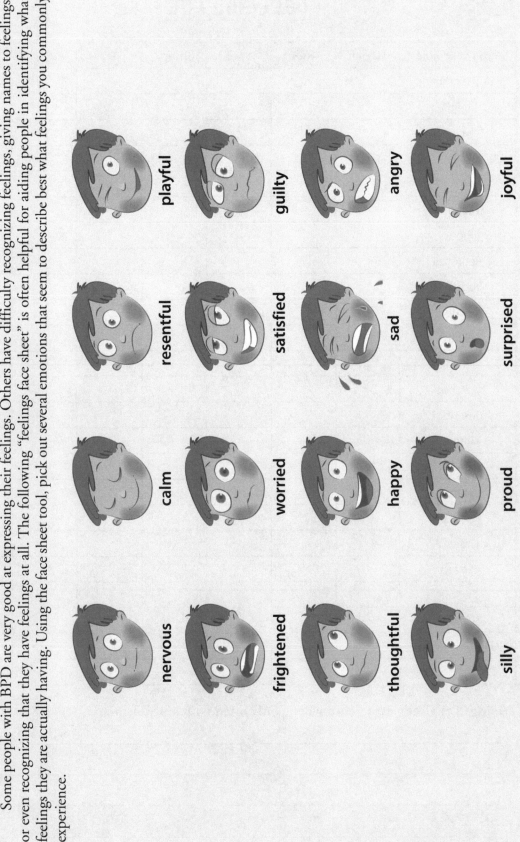

nervous	calm	resentful	playful
frightened	worried	satisfied	guilty
thoughtful	happy	sad	angry
silly	proud	surprised	joyful

Copyright 2016 © Jeff Riggenbach, *The Borderline Personality Disorder Toolbox*. All rights reserved.

FEELINGS LOG

Type of Feeling	Mon	Tues	Wed	Thurs	Fri	Sat	Sun
Happy							
Sad							
Excited							
Angry							
Irritated							
Frustrated							
Proud							
Regretful							
Disgusted							
Excited							
Guilty							
Ashamed							
Anxious							
Resentful							
Gloomy							
Fearful							
Scared							
Panicked							
Grateful							
Loved							
Envious							
Jealous							
Compassionate							
Affectionate							

Feelings I typically experience when confronted with a problem are:

1. _____

2. _____

3. _____

4. _____

Copyright 2016 © Jeff Riggenbach, *The Borderline Personality Disorder Toolbox*. All rights reserved.

IDENTIFYING TRIGGERS

A trigger is something that sets off a thought, emotion, an image or a flashback. Triggers are personal, and thus highly individualized. Triggers may be more obvious, such as when someone who has been abused as a child is yelled at as an adult and similar feelings are evoked.

But oftentimes, triggers are much more subtle: songs that come on the radio that remind you of a certain time, a whiff of perfume as you walk through the mall, or even someone's tone of voice can all trigger emotions based upon past experiences. Regardless of the type of symptoms you struggle with (anxiety, anger, depression, etc.), it is important to identify what types of things set them off.

My Triggers:

1. _____

2. _____

3. _____

4. _____

5. _____

Copyright 2016 © Jeff Riggenbach, *The Borderline Personality Disorder Toolbox*. All rights reserved.

LABELING DISTORTIONS

The term cognitive distortion sometimes turns people off. It seems to some like complicated terminology that sounds as if someone has brain damage. On the contrary, cognitive distortions are actually fairly simple to understand and, once applied, can be one of the more freeing tools for people with BPD to gain relief.

Some prefer more user-friendly terms such as "thinking errors" or "automatic negative thoughts" (ANTs). Whatever you call them, **cognitive distortions are specific types of irrational thinking**. They are not specific to people with BPD or, for that matter, to any mental illness. Every person commits cognitive distortions on a daily basis. But people with borderline personality disorder are generally more prone to misinterpret statements or events, so understanding these distortions can be vital for recovery from BPD.

Cognitive Distortions

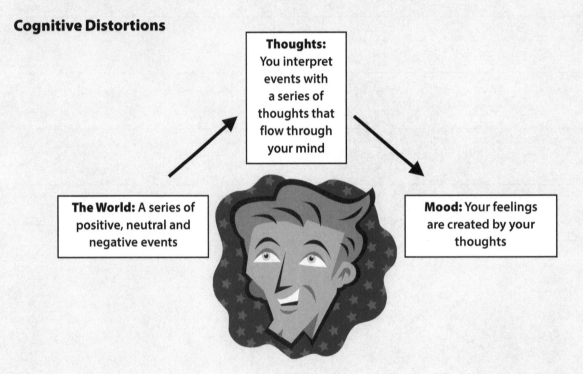

Thoughts: You interpret events with a series of thoughts that flow through your mind

The World: A series of positive, neutral and negative events

Mood: Your feelings are created by your thoughts

Our emotions result mostly from the way we *perceive events*. Before we can experience any feeling, we must process it with our minds in way that gives it meaning. The way that each person *understand*s what is happening influences how they *feel* about it. To the degree that your thinking about a given event is biased in any way, your feelings may be that much more intense, which will make it that much harder to act in a way that is helpful.

What follows are 10 misperceptions, which we will call *Cognitive Distortions*, that form the basis for emotional difficulties. (Adapted from Burns, 1990)

Copyright 2016 © Jeff Riggenbach, *The Borderline Personality Disorder Toolbox*. All rights reserved.

COGNITIVE DISTORTIONS

Use this to identify the most common distortions in your thinking.

1. **Rationalization**. In an attempt to protect yourself from hurt feelings, you create excuses for events in life which don't go your way or for poor choices you make. "It's OK for my husband to be abusive because he just doesn't know how to show his love, and besides, he only did it twice."

2. **Overgeneralization**. You see a single negative event as applicable to all or no situations. You put people or things in categories based upon your personal experience. "I've been married three times and all three men were abusive, so every man on the planet is violent."

3. **All-or-nothing thinking**. This refers to a tendency to see things in black and white categories with no consideration for grey. You see yourself, others, and often the whole world in only positive or negative extremes, rather than considering that each may instead have both positive and negative aspects. For example, if your performance falls short of perfect one time, you see yourself as a total failure.

4. **Discounting the positive**. You reject positive experiences by insisting that they "don't count" for one reason or another. In this way you can maintain a negative belief that is contradicted by your everyday experiences. You reject compliments thinking (and sometimes saying), "It's not a big deal; anyone could have done that."

5. **Fortune-telling**. You anticipate that things will turn out badly and you feel convinced that your prediction is already an established fact. This belief may result from negative experiences in the past. However, just because something ended a certain way in the past does not mean it will this time. "I know I am not going to get this job, so I will not even apply."

6. **Mind-reading**. You arbitrarily conclude that someone is reacting negatively to you, and you don't bother to check this out. This belief is based on past interactions with others, and fails to consider that each person and situation is different and unique, and that you are different now as well. "She is probably upset with me."

7. **Should statements**. You place false or unrealistic expectations on yourself or others. When we "should" others, the emotional consequence is anger ("He shouldn't be going slowly in the fast lane!"). "Shoulding" ourselves may lead to guilt ("I shouldn't have said those mean things to my mom.").

8. **Emotional reasoning**. You assume that your negative feelings reflect the way things really are. "I feel it, therefore it must be true."

9. **Magnification**. You exaggerate the importance of things such as mistakes made by you or others. This is often referred to as 'blowing things out of proportion' or catastrophizing. "I didn't get this job, so I will never get a job and my kids will die of starvation."

10. **Personalization**. You see yourself as the cause of some external negative event for which, in fact, you were not primarily responsible. "It's my fault she is unhappy."

Copyright 2016 © Jeff Riggenbach, *The Borderline Personality Disorder Toolbox*. All rights reserved.

WAIT (What Am I Thinking?)

After you have identified the distortion, the important thing is to identify the specific automatic thought behind it. Some therapists may use the term *irrational thoughts* (Ellis, 1975). Others prefer the term *dysfunctional thoughts* or *maladaptive thoughts* (Beck, 1975). The advantage of thinking of thoughts as dysfunctional is recognizing that thoughts that were functional or helpful in one setting may become dysfunctional or hurtful in other settings.

For instance, someone who grew up in an abusive family might have learned through experience that, **"If I speak up, somebody gets hit, yelled at, or leaves, so it's best that I just never speak up."** In those circumstances, if someone really did get hurt every time he opened his mouth, it would be adaptive to keep his mouth shut. But, if that person persists in that way of thinking ("It's best that I just keep my mouth shut") even after he has grown up and left that home, it is not functional or adaptive and will not lead to effective outcomes. What is functional in one setting is not necessarily helpful in other contexts.

Other professionals may use the term *distorted thinking*, which is the term used in this workbook. So, **when you catch your emotions escalating, it can be helpful to pause a moment, and use the acronym WAIT**. Don't act impulsively. Identifying your thoughts accurately is the first step to de-escalating. Use this tool to ask yourself the following questions to identify your specific thoughts. Becoming aware of thoughts and identifying them accurately is an important part of recovery.

Other helpful questions might include:

- What am I usually telling myself?
- If I were in a cartoon, what would the bubble above my head be saying?
- If there were a tape recorder in my head recording my every thought, what would it be saying when someone pushed "play?"

The next time you experience an intense emotion, write down the emotion and try to identify what your specific thoughts are.

I felt ...	because I thought...
Hurt	"Since she said that, she must not care about me."
Angry	"He should be more fair. He should try to understand me and he isn't."
Relieved	"At least I won't have to put up with that anymore."

I felt ...	because I thought...

Copyright 2016 © Jeff Riggenbach, *The Borderline Personality Disorder Toolbox*. All rights reserved.

RATIONAL RESPONDING/
CHALLENGING DISTORTED THOUGHTS

Recognizing distorted thoughts is the first step, but unfortunately, many people stop there. Recognizing our distorted thoughts, but not doing anything about them keeps us stuck. One cognitive tool you can use is *CHALLENGING* your distorted thoughts. **Challenging means that you are "arguing" with the actual content of the thought.**

Challenging distorted thoughts doesn't always make them go away, but it can put up enough of a "fight" to lessen the intensity of the emotion you are experiencing and may be at least slightly easier to use some of your skills. You may also hear this referred to as "self-talk." Utilize the following *thought log tool* to attempt to *challenge* the distorted thoughts or generate some more *rational responses* to them. An example will help get you started.

Distorted Thought	Rational Response(s)
"Since she said that, she *must* not care about me"	" She might not have meant it like it sounded to me." " Is there any other evidence that she cares about me?" " What things has she done in the last month that might say she does care?" " Maybe she didn't mean it to sound so direct." " Even if she did, sometimes I need people to be direct with me or I don't hear them." " I could ask her to clarify what she means. She is too good a friend to lose over a possible misinterpretation."

Thought Log

Distorted Thought	Rational Response(s)

Copyright 2016 © Jeff Riggenbach, *The Borderline Personality Disorder Toolbox*. All rights reserved.

EXCUSES ARE LIKE ARMPITS

Different cognitive distortions require challenging in specifically different ways. The first distortion is called rationalization. You may have heard the old axiom *excuses are like armpits: we all have a couple of them, and they stink!*

Rationalization is really a fancy word for making excuses. When we rationalize our own behavior, we are giving ourselves permission to do something that is in some way harmful to us.

When we rationalize someone else's behavior, we are giving them permission to do something that is in some way harmful to us. So rationalizations always take the form of one of the following:

Self-Rationalization: "It's OK to _____ because _____."
behavior   excuse

Other Rationalization: "It's OK that he/she did _____
behavior

because_____."
excuse

Examples:

"It's OK to yell at him because he yelled at me first."

"It's OK to binge because I have to feel in control of something."

"It's OK to cut because then he will see how much pain I am really in and be there for me more."

"It's OK for him to abuse me because it isn't too bad and I can't be alone."

"It's OK for her to treat me poorly because I don't deserve any better."

Use the following to help you identify some behaviors you have struggled with in the recent past or continue to engage in and identify the reason/excuse you give yourself for engaging in it.

"It's OK to _____ because _____."

"It's OK to _____ because _____."

"It's OK to _____ because _____."

Copyright 2016 © Jeff Riggenbach, *The Borderline Personality Disorder Toolbox*. All rights reserved.

Turn on your Dimmer Switch

Black and white thinking or all or nothing thinking is a cognitive distortion. The technical cognitive term is dichotomous thinking. This is very similar to the Freudian concept of "splitting." Black and white thinkers see things in extremes. This polarized thinking creates difficulty experiencing "middle ground" mood states.

Black and white thinking prevents people from seeing things in shades of grey. Think of those rooms that do not simply have an "off" / "on" switch, but have a dimmer switch. This is a great analogy for what black and white thinking is – a room with an "off" / "on" switch only.

There is no 'dimmer switch' that allows BPD individuals to see all those shades of grey in between "completely on" and "completely off." Awareness is the first step. It is often helpful to journal how often you catch yourself thinking in extreme terms. Keep track each day how many times you catch yourself saying or thinking the following. Tally the number of your frequent phrases.

- "The best"
- "The worst"
- "Loves"
- "Hates"
- "Always"
- "Never"

One of the more helpful tools for people with black and white thinking is what is called a cognitive continuum. When you catch yourself using some of this extreme language, try using a continuum. Continuums work by first identifying the two opposite polar ends of the spectrum and then attempting to find some points in between.

Example: "I hate my dad. He is the worst person in the world!"

Mother Teresa   Aunt Jenny   friend Jo   Dad   Hitler   Saddam Hussein

|----------------------|----------------|------------|------------|--------------------|

Best Person   **Worst Person**
in the World   **in the World**

Try some continuums of your own when you catch yourself using extremes. Try to find some points representing middle ground and see if you can turn on your dimmer switch!

Cognitive Distortion: _____

|----------------------|----------------|------------|------------|--------------------|

Copyright 2016 © Jeff Riggenbach, *The Borderline Personality Disorder Toolbox*. All rights reserved.

Cognitive Distortion: _____

|----------------------|---------------|-----------|-----------|------------------|

Cognitive Distortion: _____

|----------------------|---------------|-----------|-----------|------------------|

Cognitive Distortion: _____

|----------------------|---------------|-----------|-----------|------------------|

Copyright 2016 © Jeff Riggenbach, *The Borderline Personality Disorder Toolbox*. All rights reserved.

ACCEPTING COMPLIMENTS

Deep down no person with BPD likes themselves very much. There are no exceptions. It is a symptom of the condition. Because of that, it is very difficult for people with BPD to accept compliments. Discounting the positives maintains their negative beliefs about themselves. As long as they continue to do this, they will stay stuck and not get better. Positives might include compliments, positive attributes, successful task completion, or other positive experiences.

A previous therapist may have instructed you to smile and say, "thank you," when someone gives you a compliment. For some, this seems to help. For others, it does not. Probably what you "tell yourself" as you say "thank you" has a lot to do with whether this helps you or not. For instance, some people smile and say, "thank you," but are simultaneously telling themselves:

- "He is full of it."
- "He is just saying that."
- "I don't believe her at all."
- "That might be true for other people, but it doesn't count for me."

Some even have thoughts like:

- "I know what she wants me to say, so if I just say thank you she will stop bugging me."

Having these thoughts while you are saying "thank you" likely stops any new information from "getting in," so your self-esteem doesn't change. More helpful thoughts might include:

- "I don't believe it, but I'm really going to try to believe it."
- "Consider the source – does that person usually tell me things that aren't true?"
- "I know I don't often see good in myself – here is a chance to work at getting better."

Another helpful way to use the tool of accepting compliments is to take a compliment someone has given you (i.e., "you were so thoughtful") and look *purposefully* for that trait. Some people even keep a log at the end of every day writing down times when they did something that was thoughtful. Plan to behave thoughtfully. Monitor yourself. Give yourself credit when you do. As you build this "muscle memory" you will more easily be able say thank you and mean it the next time someone calls you thoughtful.

Describe ways you will work on accepting compliments:

_____

_____

_____

_____

_____

_____

Copyright 2016 © Jeff Riggenbach, *The Borderline Personality Disorder Toolbox*. All rights reserved.

SELF-ESTEEM BUILDING

Due to the unhealthy core beliefs and difficulty accepting compliments, it is difficult for people with BPD to build self-esteem. Use this tool to **write a descriptive complimentary word that starts with each letter of the alphabet**. Get a friend or therapist to do it with you!

A _____

B _____

C _____

D _____

E _____

F _____

G _____

H _____

I _____

J _____

K _____

L _____

M _____

N _____

O _____

P _____

Q _____

R _____

S _____

T _____

U _____

V _____

W _____

X _____

Y _____

Z _____

Copyright 2016 © Jeff Riggenbach, *The Borderline Personality Disorder Toolbox*. All rights reserved.

Adding a But

Hearing compliments can sometimes be difficult, particularly if they don't fit one of your negative beliefs about yourself. One way to work on developing more healthy beliefs is by using the "add a but" tool (Beck, 2005).

The way this one works is that every time you receive a compliment or have a positive experience and your distorted thinking kicks in and says, "Yes, but …," you write the "negative but" down and then add a "positive but"—something positive or healthy to counter the "negative but." You can do this with any affirmations or compliments you receive from day to day.

Positive Attribute/Skill	Discounting "But"	Add a "But"
I can be kind	I snapped at my husband last night	I also cooked him dinner and did his laundry

Add a But Log:

Positive Attribute/Skill	Discounting "But"	Add a "But"

Copyright 2016 © Jeff Riggenbach, *The Borderline Personality Disorder Toolbox*. All rights reserved.

ABOLISHING ASSUMPTIONS

Fortune-telling and mind-reading are similar thought distortions and are common with Borderline Personality Disorder. Colloquially, people call these the "what-ifs?," "What if this happens?," "What if that happens?" and "What if she's thinking this?" "What if he does that?" These distortions fuel anxiety and lead to avoidant behaviors.

Research has shown that 90 percent of the things we worry about never happen (Leahy, 2004). Additionally, when that worst case scenario really does happen, 80 percent of the time, people say, "I handled it better than I thought I could." That's what fortune-telling and mind-reading do. They cause you to *overestimate* risk and *underestimate* your ability to cope. Challenging fortune-telling and mind-reading involves **reminding yourself of the resources or abilities you really do have in order to face whatever situation is causing you to be anxious, and then re-evaluating the risk** ("What is the real likelihood of this?").

Use the thought log below to identify some of your fortune-telling or mind-reading thoughts and then challenge them using statements affirming your abilities, your resources, or re-evaluating the risk.

Fortune-Telling or Mind-Reading Thought (Negative Assumption)	Rational Responses/Challenges
I will never pass this course. "It is graduate level and I am not smart enough."	"I have a good chance to pass this course." "I have never failed an entire course in my life." "My GPA indicates that I am smart." "Sheena passed it last semester and I know I am smarter than her." "They offer tutoring - if I need help I can get it."

Copyright 2016 © Jeff Riggenbach, *The Borderline Personality Disorder Toolbox*. All rights reserved.

Face your Fears

Sometimes, it is not enough to cognitively convince yourself of the likelihood of something: it is necessary to *experience* being safe in a situation you predicted would be dangerous. The only way to do this is to face your fears.

Anxiety is developed and perpetuated by believing something is more threatening than it really is and by minimizing our ability to cope with that perceived or actual threat. Many people who struggle with anxiety have experienced actual danger in their lives. Many people with BPD have been hurt physically or emotionally. But not all people who have been hurt struggle with anxiety. Anxiety persists when we continue to view threats as currently present even when, in reality, they may not be. It is common for people to cope by using what are called *safety behaviors*.

Safety behaviors are any behaviors that decrease anxiety in the short term (so the person feels "safe") but, in actuality, make the anxiety worse in the long term. One of the most important steps for overcoming anxiety is identifying and eliminating safety behaviors. Many say, "If I give up my safety net, I'll become more anxious." **The only way to truly help your anxiety get better in the long run is to retrain your brain to recognize that things you once thought were dangerous are not and that you are generally safer than you previously believed—or that the actual threat isn't nearly as great as you previously thought.** The reality is that 90 percent of the things we worry about never happen. Safety behaviors block the brain from learning this crucial lesson.

Most people are not aware that safety behaviors are harmful, and many do not even recognize they are doing them. Therefore, identifying your safety behaviors is an important first step. Use the following to help you consider behaviors you may be doing that help you feel less anxious in the short term, but that may be keeping you from being able to test your fear-based beliefs.

Example Safety Behaviors

- Taking stairs instead of elevators
- Having a drink before every social event to "loosen up"
- Driving instead of flying
- Checking the door 10 times before going to bed every night
- Going to early church service because few other people there
- Shopping at 2 am
- Using a driving route that takes 30 extra minutes so as not to have to cross a bridge
- Not initiating conversation
- Never going shopping for fear of overspending
- Changing the subject when asked about something uncomfortable

In my previous book, *The CBT Toolbox*, I shared some examples from Dr. Martin Antony's *The Anti-Anxiety Handbook* that list some safety behaviors common for specific conditions, which you might want to consider when compiling your own list of safety behaviors. This book is an excellent resource if anxiety is mostly what you struggle with.

Copyright 2016 © Jeff Riggenbach, *The Borderline Personality Disorder Toolbox*. All rights reserved.

Anxiety Problem or Diagnosis	Common Safety Behaviors
Panic disorder and agoraphobia	• Sitting in aisle seat in theatre to facilitate quick escape • Always having a "safe" person around when going to feared situations • Frequently checking pulse to ensure heart is not racing • Sitting down and resting when panic begins
Social anxiety and shyness	• Wearing make-up to hide blushing • Wearing light clothing to hide sweating in public • Over-preparing for presentations • Avoiding eye contact when talking to others
Generalized anxiety and worry	• Leaving home extra early for appointments so there is no chance of being late • Phoning children frequently to make sure they are OK • Not buying things you can easily afford for fear someday you may have no money
Obsessive-compulsive issues	• Wearing gloves when touching things that may be "contaminated" • Excessive hand washing • Repeated checking to make sure work is done correctly
Anxiety from past trauma	• Carrying pepper spray to protect yourself from possible assault • Driving extra slowly to avoid a car accident • Walking with your back to the wall in public to prevent being attacked
Phobias related to blood and needles	• Lying down during blood test to avoid becoming faint • Looking away during blood draw
Phobias related to animals	• Checking for dogs through window before going for a walk • Carrying an umbrella to protect self from harmless snakes
Other specific phobias	• Flying business class to avoid feeling closed in • Driving only in the right lane to make it easy to pull over if necessary • Over-preparing for tests or exams

My Safety Behaviors

In 1999, David Satcher, then U. S. Surgeon General, wrote perhaps the most complete review of mental health and treatment ever published (Satcher, 1999). In it, he stated that the most important and critical part of treatment for anxiety is "exposure to stimuli"; in other words, facing your fears.

You may have heard the term *exposure*. Exposure is probably the most important strategy for recovery. Unfortunately, it can also be the most difficult because it requires you to do the things you fear the most. It's one thing to *tell* yourself something isn't as scary as you thought it was. It's another thing to *prove* it to yourself. Exposure-based strategies are based on the principle that we all get used to things over time.

Copyright 2016 © Jeff Riggenbach, *The Borderline Personality Disorder Toolbox*. All rights reserved.

Although extremely effective when done correctly, exposure therapy can often be harmful if not done properly, so it is best that you plan this series of exercises with your therapist. As you plan to face your fears, remember one thing: The goal is not to do the exercise without experiencing any anxiety. The goal is to test your belief to see if your fearful perceptions are true. If they aren't true as you *experience* this over time, your brain learns to process threat differently and your anxiety will decrease. Anxiety typically decreases with gradual exposure over time, so be patient. Occasionally (but rarely), catastrophic beliefs do turn out to be true. If this is the case, do not fear! The tool discussed next will help you cope with this situation.

Another helpful tool from *The Anti-Anxiety Handbook* (pp 157–159, with permission) to help you work with exposure is the following exposure log:

Example Exposure Log

Date	Belief	Pre-test (%)	Test	Result	Post-test (%)
6/13	Bridge will collapse if I go over it	95	Visualize driving over bridge	Made it safely, bridge didn't collapse	90
6/15		90	Watch other cars drive over bridge	55 cars crossed safely in one hour; none fell through	80
6/17		80	Drove over bridge myself first time	Made it safely; bridge didn't collapse	60

My Exposure Log

Date	Belief	Pre-test (%)	Test	Result	Post-test (%)

Copyright 2016 © Jeff Riggenbach, *The Borderline Personality Disorder Toolbox*. All rights reserved.

FACE THE FACTS

Should statements are perhaps the most difficult of the thought distortions for many people to cope with, not just people with Borderline Personality Disorder. However, because anger and guilt are primary emotions associated with BPD, these distortions are especially important for individuals with personality disorders to pay attention to. First, it is important to note that there are two types of "shoulds". As presented earlier, you can "should" other people, so to speak, or you can "should" yourself. Should statements have everything to do with our expectations. So, when we expect other people to behave a certain way and they do not, we "should" them and get angry. When you do not live up to your own expectations for yourself, you should yourself and feel guilty.

Should statements are distorted because they have nothing to do with reality. They have only to do with how we think something should be. There are also a lot of shoulds in disguise. For instance you may catch yourself using words like *ought to, must, supposed to, has to, needs to*. These are all in the should family and can lead to the emotion of anger. Since anger is a symptom of BPD, and all anger comes from shoulds, the better handle we can get on this way of thinking, the less we will suffer from this emotion.

Since shoulds are irrational because they have nothing to do with reality, the way to challenge shoulds is through simple reality-based statements. Linehan talks about a concept called *Radical Acceptance*. But before Linehan ever got acceptance mainstreamed in psychotherapy, Albert Ellis (1977), Aaron Beck (1980), Bob Leahy (1991) and others were helping patients become less angry by accepting reality. Leahy calls it *moral resistance* when we continue to insist some aspect of reality *shouldn't* be the way that it is.

As long as we continue to process information in that manner (think that way), we will continue to stay angry. It is that simple. If we are angry, we have one or more should statements going through our minds towards someone or something else. Use the following thought log to challenge your shoulds. Some examples are given.

Should Statement	Reality/Acceptance-Based Challenge
"He shouldn't watch so much ESPN – I can't believe he's watching sports again instead of spending time with me."	<ul><li>He is watching ESPN.</li><li>He has always liked sports.</li><li>There are times I spend time doing things I like… and it doesn't mean I don't want to be with him.</li><li>There are worse things husbands do with their time.</li><li>I can ask him and we can plan to do something together later.</li><li>My getting upset is only going to make things worse.</li><li>I can use this time to go work on enjoying something for myself alone.</li></ul>

Copyright 2016 © Jeff Riggenbach, *The Borderline Personality Disorder Toolbox*. All rights reserved.

Should Statement	Reality/Acceptance-Based Challenge
"My uncle shouldn't have abused me sexually – he ruined my life. I will hate him forever!"	"I wish he hadn't done that. It has affected my life severely. But he did. I can't change it now. All I can do is move forward. If I hate him forever, he will continue to have power over my emotions and my life, and I will not give that to him. I choose to accept the past and live in freedom for my future."

Use the thought log below to challenge some of your should statements.

Should Statement	Reality/Acceptance-Based Challenge

Copyright 2016 © Jeff Riggenbach, *The Borderline Personality Disorder Toolbox*. All rights reserved.

Desensitizing yourself to Guilt Stabs

Do you have those people in your life who know just the right thing to say to make you feel guilty? Those statements have often been referred to as "guilt stabs." Many people with borderline personality disorder are susceptible to guilt. But have you ever noticed that guilt stabs don't seem to work on some people? How could that be? Actually, some people don't feel guilty in situations where some amount of guilt would actually be warranted. That is unhealthy in a different way. "Should statements" are always connected to our values. So when others violate our values, we "should" them and feel angry. When we violate our own values, we "should" ourselves and feel guilty. But again, because of those negative core beliefs, people with BPD are typically extremely vulnerable to the guilt stab.

How exactly does it work? What the beliefs (or filters) do is assign blame. People with negative self-beliefs blame themselves *even when such blame is not warranted*. So if this is the case for you, it is likely true that people in your life have learned the right "buttons to push" (the right things to say) to influence you to feel guilty and do whatever it is they want you to do. We will talk about "desensitizing your buttons" in a later tool, but for now, when you feel guilt specifically, here are some questions to ask yourself:

- "What is my should statement toward myself?"
- "What value of mine did I really violate?"
- "Did I really do anything wrong?"

If you are able to identify a value of yours that you violated (and you really did do something wrong), some guilt is *healthy*. Forgive yourself, ask others to forgive you, if necessary, and use the conviction to motivate you to *change your behavior* in the future to live consistently with your values.

If you didn't do anything wrong, then your guilt is *unhealthy*. Do not beat yourself up. Do not apologize. Do not change your behavior. Rather work to *change your thinking*. Remind yourself that you did nothing wrong. You may feel guilty out of habit. Perhaps you had a parent who was critical and you have internalized an idea like, "Someone is upset with me; I must have done something wrong." We all make mistakes. Sometimes guilt is healthy. Oftentimes it is not. Be accountable for things that are your responsibility. But do not take responsibility for what is not. Challenge sternly those shoulds that beat you up. Use the thought log below to challenge some of your shoulds. Keep working on this, and you will feel less guilty over time.

Self Should	Rational Responses

Copyright 2016 © Jeff Riggenbach, *The Borderline Personality Disorder Toolbox*. All rights reserved.

IF IT FEELS GOOD, DO IT...NOT

In the 1980s, it was popular to say "NOT" when something was a bad idea or you disagreed with something. Acting on emotions is a common problem for many people with BPD and it is almost never a good idea. The distortion of emotional reasoning says, "If I feel this way, it is this way."

There are self-help books that encourage "trust your heart" or "go with your intuition." The problem is, they are encouraging people to act on their emotions which can be influenced by distorted thinking.

After all, you could put 10 people in the identical situation and you could have 10 different "intuitions" as to what to do. . . and at least nine of them could be wrong! Use the following tool to list three ways you could make a decision without using emotional reasoning.

An Example:

- Ask 3 other people whose judgment I trust
- Wait at least 24 hours before acting and make sure my decision is the same tomorrow
- Weigh the pros and cons

1. _____

_____

2. _____

_____

3. _____

_____

Copyright 2016 © Jeff Riggenbach, *The Borderline Personality Disorder Toolbox*. All rights reserved.

IT'S NOT ALL ABOUT YOU

Personalization is one of the most problematic thought distortions for people with BPD. The natural tendency is to make statements or comments *MEAN* something negative about them that they usually do not mean.

It is important to remember what these negative self-beliefs do – they distort meaning. As a result of these perceptual problems, individuals with BPD get their feelings hurt a heck of a lot more than most people. They are very sensitive to criticism and rejection. Many comments that were not intended to be personal or hurtful are perceived that way by the individual with BPD.

So, when your feelings get hurt, it can be important to make sure you aren't over-personalizing something. Personalization challenges usually include responses like:

- "Was that really about me?"
- "Is there anything else he could have meant?"
- "Is there another way to take this?"
- "Possibly this means something about someone else."
- "Maybe it means nothing."
- "I can check it out with them later."

Use the following thought log to identify and challenge your personalization thoughts:

Personalization Thoughts	Rational Responses/Challenges
"Because I did not get an invitation to the birthday party in the mail, it must mean he doesn't like me."	"Maybe he didn't send out invitations." "Maybe he is late sending them out and I could still get one." "Maybe it is for family only." "Just because I didn't get an invite doesn't mean he doesn't like me."

Copyright 2016 © Jeff Riggenbach, *The Borderline Personality Disorder Toolbox*. All rights reserved.

DOUBLE STANDARD

All people with BPD struggle with very self-critical thoughts. In addition to discounting the positive, individuals with BPD take this a step further. Not only can they not take in positive information, they often beat themselves up with negative, critical thoughts.

Do you ever feel like you just get up in the morning and get that big metaphorical guilt club out from underneath your bed and start beating yourself over the head with it? How does that affect your mood? **While some people are just as critical of others as they are themselves, most judge themselves more harshly than they judge others.**

The double standard technique asks you to examine this idea. For instance, have you ever lost a job or a relationship and had thoughts toward yourself such as, "I can't do anything right," or, "I am such a loser." How do those thoughts make you feel?

The double standard technique asks you to identify a good friend or family member you care about and ask yourself, "If they went through the same thing, would I be thinking the same harsh/judging thoughts towards them?" If your answer is no, you are judging yourself more harshly than you would judge them, and you are not being objective and fair with yourself. You are viewing the situation in a biased manner and using a double standard. It is important to be intellectually honest. If you wouldn't judge someone else that harshly for the same event, it is not fair to judge yourself that harshly either!

A variation of this that we do in our group program is what we call the "degree of sin" exercise. When someone is beating themselves up for something they did wrong (actual or perceived), we will ask them, "On a scale of 0-10, how big of a 'sin' do you believe this is?" The individual will give their subjective rating. Then, we ask each group member to give their subjective rating. For instance, while doing this exercise in group last week, the person we were working with rated her sin a "9", but everyone else in the group rated it a "4" or below. The individual was then able to make the statement, **"Wow, maybe I do need to cut myself a little slack."**

Oftentimes, every member of the group may agree that a member's behavior was wrong or unhelpful, but the consensus is usually that the person's degree of judgment is neither appropriate to the situation nor healthy. On some occasions, after processing with the group, members will come to the conclusion that what they did was not even wrong in any way, so no judgment was even warranted.

Use the table on the following page as a tool for assessing the fairness of your standards.

Copyright 2016 © Jeff Riggenbach, *The Borderline Personality Disorder Toolbox*. All rights reserved.

STANDARD FAIRNESS

Situation or behavior	Self-critical thoughts	Degree of sin	Advice I'd give a friend	Degree of sin (if it were them)
Took ex-boyfriend back	"You are so stupid." "You are such a loser."	8	Leaving an abusive relationship is hard – just get a new plan and try again.	2

Copyright 2016 © Jeff Riggenbach, *The Borderline Personality Disorder Toolbox*. All rights reserved.

Becoming "Good Enough" & Dealing with Perfectionism

Many people with borderline personality disorder have developed unrealistic standards for themselves (and sometimes others). Some people's childhoods involved constantly being corrected, criticized, and evaluated. Over time, this message of being "not good enough" leads to internalization of a belief that one must be perfect.

The desire to meet high standards or achieve goals is healthy. But the desire to be perfect is unhealthy. No human being is perfect. Believing we "should" be is setting ourselves up for failure, and the depression, stress, and frustration that accompany it. Perfectionism can cause psychological distress (stress, depression, anger), inhibit work performance, and damage (if not permanently destroy) relationships. **Use the following tool to help identify some of your perfectionistic thoughts and behaviors; then list some alternatives that you could use to believe that you are "good enough."**

Rational Response Log Example:

	EVENT	THOUGHTS	FEELINGS	ACTIONS	RESULTS
Automatic Thoughts	Boyfriend arrived five minutes late	"I am never late; he shouldn't be late. Since he is always late, he is disrespectful."	Angry	Yell at him. Criticize him.	We get in a fight. He criticizes me. I hate him. I hate me. I am in a tizzy all week.
Rational Responses	Boyfriend arrived five minutes late	"Even though I am usually on time, I am late once in a while." "Just because he is late doesn't mean he disrespects me. He was late before he met me; his lateness has nothing to do with me." "I have plenty of weaknesses, too. I want him to show me grace with mine, so I need to show him grace with his."	A little irritated, but less angry.	Bite my tongue. Comment on it later when we are talking calmly.	We get along. No fighting. No intense, unpleasant emotions.

Copyright 2016 © Jeff Riggenbach, *The Borderline Personality Disorder Toolbox*. All rights reserved.

Choose the perfectionistic dysfunctional thought you identify with the most. Plug it, as well as your rational challenges to it, into the sequential log:

	EVENT	THOUGHTS	FEELINGS	ACTIONS	RESULTS
Automatic Thoughts					
Rational Responses					

Copyright 2016 © Jeff Riggenbach, *The Borderline Personality Disorder Toolbox*. All rights reserved.

TAKE THAT (GIVE UP THE NEED TO PUNISH)

An unfortunate hallmark quality of the borderline personality disordered individual is a need to punish people, or "get them back" for one reason or another. Here are some common BPD cognitions related to the punitive belief:

- "Since he didn't understand me, I'll show him!"
- "Since she didn't take me seriously, I'll show her!"
- "Since they hurt me, I'll hurt them worse!"
- "Since they didn't give me what they should have, I'll get them back!"

Punishing can help one feel self-righteous in the moment and can even provide a feeling of momentary relief by knowing, "at least they got theirs." But long-term, these behaviors always backfire as well. They make others not like us, which, in turn, leads to them withdrawing, which causes further feelings of hurt and rejection. **Below, consider some punishing behaviors you have engaged in that have not worked so well, and list some alternative behaviors you are willing to try. An example is listed.**

Punishing Behavior	Past Negative Results	New Coping Skill
Fabricated a story to get an ex- lover fired	Guilt from knowing I did the wrong thing Hurt my spiritual life - not the kind of person I wanted to be Hurt my recovery - I tried to convince myself I did the right thing - and then detached so I would not have to feel the feelings from doing something I knew was wrong	Apologize to my ex and come clean Restore at least a civil friendship No longer listen to sick people in my life who I have been allowing to influence my behaviors Forgive myself for the past and give myself some grace Commit to do the right thing from here on

Copyright 2016 © Jeff Riggenbach, *The Borderline Personality Disorder Toolbox*. All rights reserved.

TAKING RESPONSIBILITY:
KILL THE "VICTIM MENTALITY"

Due to a history of many years of feeling invalidated, many individuals with BPD attempt to gain validation at any cost. One method some use is to play the victim.

While many patients with borderline personality disorder have been *victimized*, not all of them take on this *victim mentality*. While the motive is typically a desperate attempt to feel understood, these behaviors often backfire, and rub others the wrong way (oftentimes infuriating the BPD individual who then ups the ante to get noticed, which escalates the situation). Some common strategies engaged in by those with victim mentalities trying to feel validated include:

- Obsessing about how "awful" life is
- Escalating their intensity
- Surrounding self with "awfulizing" friends
- Splitting behaviors
- Self-invalidating statements/self-put-downs

It is NORMAL to want to be validated. Every human being needs validation. But it is important to learn to seek it in healthier ways. Playing the victim never works long term to facilitate recovery. Use the tool below to identify some of the victim behaviors you have employed in the past and list healthier alternative coping skills you could try:

Victim Behaviors	Alternate Coping Skills
Telling others how bad I have it and constantly saying "you don't understand" Not trying things Demanding that others owe you	Be around people who will validate you Stop expecting to get needs met from people who can't/won't meet them Try things even if I believe I can't - I won't know until I try I will never get what i want demanding - the best way is to earn things myself - I can use others to help but nobody owes me

Copyright 2016 © Jeff Riggenbach, *The Borderline Personality Disorder Toolbox*. All rights reserved.

Forgiveness

Unforgiveness is experienced by many as a spiritual word. It means essentially the same thing as resentment, which might be considered an emotional word. But they both refer to *anger that we hold onto over time.*

People with BPD often struggle with the concept of forgiveness.

One reason for this is that the thought process of the individual with BPD inherently struggles with "shoulds" and "punishing" types of cognitions, which are incompatible with forgiveness. **Forgiveness has been associated with a number of benefits related to emotional well-being as well as physical health.** Entire books have been devoted to the topic of forgiveness. If this is an idea you struggle with, you may want to get one of these books. Talking with a religious counselor who is somewhat versed in mental health issues can often be helpful as well. This tool will help you look at several distorted thoughts often related to difficulty starting this process of forgiveness.

Myth: "*Forgive and Forget.*" This is a nifty little saying. Hopefully, we are able to forget smaller matters. Some hurts, however, run deep. Many people with BPD have been wounded in very severe and personal ways that can never be forgotten. In response to hearing the phrase "forgive and forget" many people respond with versions of, "if I have to forget to forgive, I can never forgive."

Truth: It is NOT necessary to forget to forgive. We will never forget some things in life. Sometimes it is healthy NOT to forget. People who forget altogether often fail to learn from situations and tend to be re-victimized. It is not necessary to forget an event in order to choose not to continue to spend energy harboring a grudge against someone.

Myth: "*Time heals all wounds*"

Truth: If time really healed all wounds, nobody would go to their grave angry, and we all know people who have done that. If time healed all wounds, all people would eventually forgive, and we have people in this country still angry about what happened to their ancestors generations ago. If time healed all wounds, when that magical amount of time has passed, anger would dissipate. *The reality is that we can all choose to hold a grudge as long as we want to.* Time can be helpful to give us the distance from the offense to be able to think about it differently than we did at the time it occurred, but the reality is forgiveness takes *work* on our part. We must actively participate in this process. If we say, "I'll forgive him/her when I feel like it," we will never get around to taking the initiative we need to take.

Myth: "*Forgiveness happens overnight.*" Well-meaning clergy have said versions of, "If you forgive today, all your anger will be gone tomorrow and you will never feel it again."

Truth: For smaller offenses, this often can occur. But for deeper wounds, forgiveness is a process. It takes time and it takes work. Feelings of anger may gradually continue to come and go throughout your process of learning to let go. Just because you still feel anger, doesn't mean forgiveness isn't possible and it certainly doesn't mean that forgiveness isn't worth it.

Copyright 2016 © Jeff Riggenbach, *The Borderline Personality Disorder Toolbox*. All rights reserved.

Myth: "*Forgiveness = Trust.*" You may also have well-meaning people in your life who say things like "Well if you have truly forgiven me, you will trust me again," or, "If you really forgave him, you should be able to take him back."

Truth: Forgiveness is about the past. Trust is about the future. It is completely possible to let go of wrongs from the past, but choose not to resume a relationship in the present (or future). All major religions teach the importance of forgiveness. Forgiveness is always healthy. Trust is not always healthy. It is not healthy to continue to trust untrustworthy people. It is completely healthy to forgive someone, but choose never to trust them in certain situations.

Myth: "*Forgiveness is for them.*"

Truth: Some people erroneously think, "If I forgive him/her I am letting them off the hook." In some way, they believe that holding onto their anger is somehow hurting the offender. Some people are holding grudges against someone who wronged them 20 years ago, and that person hasn't thought about the offense since it happened. Sometimes, our offenders don't even believe they wronged us in the first place! Many people are still resentful towards people who are now dead. It probably isn't hurting them, wherever they are! It may be helpful to remember the axiom, "Unforgiveness is like swallowing a drop of poison every day waiting for the other person to die." Use the following tool to identify and challenge some of your distorted thoughts related to forgiveness. You may want to discuss them with your therapist or religious counselor.

Distorted Thoughts about Forgiveness	Rational Responses

Copyright 2016 © Jeff Riggenbach, *The Borderline Personality Disorder Toolbox*. All rights reserved.

COUNT YOUR BLESSINGS

You might have heard your grandmother sometimes say with a nasally, whiney tone of voice, "count your blessings." This phrase is like nails on a chalkboard for many with BPD as it often *sounds* invalidating. It *sounds* to many as though the person is saying, "just focus on the positive." It *feels* as though they are ignoring your pain, and it reinforces *to you* that they have no idea what you are going through. Believe it or not, these statements often trigger acting out in some people with BPD. They have the thought, "She doesn't see how much I hurt – I'll show her how much I hurt!"

The truth is that, however invalidating these statements may feel (and the person who said it may indeed have no idea what they are talking about), there really is some pretty strong (and mounting) evidence supporting the role of gratitude in improving depression and despondent moods. So, rather than hear this as an edict annoyingly and dismissively spouted off by your great aunt, think of blessings as a tool in your toolbox to help combat negative feelings in yourself.

I will never forget one of our patients who got shot by a police officer (while high and trying to steal a cop car) and lost both eyes. His attitude is truly more thankful than that of most people I encounter. He is famous in our program for saying:

"I never truly saw things clearly until God took my eyes from me – it's the biggest blessing of my life." *It is all a matter of perspective and how we look at things.*

When you are in a decent mood (when you are down is NOT the time to do this - you likely won't be able to generate any positives), list some "blessings" in your life upon which you can focus during times when you get down. Some areas to focus on might include: friends, children, food, water, shelter, God, kind strangers, pets, supportive family members, church, support groups, eyesight, other senses, nature, the internet, smart phones, animals, hobbies, time alone.

My Blessings/Gratitude List

1. _____

2. _____

3. _____

4. _____

5. _____

6. _____

7. _____

8. _____

Copyright 2016 © Jeff Riggenbach, *The Borderline Personality Disorder Toolbox*. All rights reserved.

DISSOCIATION STRATEGIES

Clinical dissociation is a symptom of Borderline Personality Disorder. Dissociation may be viewed on a continuum. The reality is that we all dissociate a little bit. Have you ever been driving along and just miss an exit because your mind was somewhere else? Have you ever been sitting in a class or sermon or lecture and just "miss" parts of what was shared? We all have times we just "space out" and miss what is happening in the moment. People with BPD are just more prone to this "zoning out" than most, especially when they are *stressed* or *angry*.

So, if you find yourself missing time, the first thing to do is to slow down and do anything possible to decrease your stress level. The less stressed you are feeling, the less you will dissociate. **Anything that helps you focus on your *external world* can be helpful for detaching from emotional pain/stress.**

One exercise that many of our patients find helpful utilizes senses. We call it the Five, Five, Five exercise. As you are present, focus on and say out loud five things you *see,* five things you *hear* and five things you *feel.* You can also incorporate things you can smell or taste (if you have some snack food handy).

Other grounding techniques that involve visualizations, mantras, and even taking your shoes off can help with dissociation, as well. Finally, for those who lose time with some regularity, keeping a regular schedule or calendar can be helpful to keep track of time. Setting alarms on your cell phone or other electronic device can help, if you are prone to missing appointments.

My Dissociation Strategies
1. _____
2. _____
3. _____
4. _____
5. _____

Copyright 2016 © Jeff Riggenbach, *The Borderline Personality Disorder Toolbox.* All rights reserved.

COGNITIVE BEHAVIOR CHAIN ANALYSIS

Because of the ego-syntonic nature of personality-related issues, "blind spots" keep many people from recognizing important events in life that trigger, or escalate, their episodes. **The use of a Behavior Chain can be important in helping link various self-harmful behaviors to specific environmental events.**

Once you can identify "triggering" events that contribute to episodes escalating to the point of destructive behaviors, it can be easier to trace thoughts, feelings, and behaviors (links in the chain) from *that* point. This is often described by individuals with BPD as one of the most powerful tools they learn. Pick a *SPECIFIC* incident of recent impulsive or destructive behavior, and analyze it asking the following questions:

Incident: _____

When did the problem begin? _____

Who was I with? _____

What did they say? _____

What was I feeling? _____

What was I thinking? _____

What did I do next? _____

Then what? _____

What happened as a result of my actions? _____

What was I thinking immediately after I did it? _____

How did I feel? _____

Copyright 2016 © Jeff Riggenbach, *The Borderline Personality Disorder Toolbox*. All rights reserved.

At each link in the chain, identify three things you could have done differently (i.e., alternative thoughts or actions);

Link 1:

_____

_____

Link 2:

_____

_____

Link 3:

_____

_____

Link 4:

_____

_____

Link 5:

_____

_____

One of the valuable things about cognitive behavior chains is their ability to help people with BPD recognize the steps that can be taken at different places in the sequence of the events. Episodes often feel like 'one huge nightmare.' But it can be helpful for people to recognize that an "episode" is really a sequence of events; often, people realize that they had more options to think or act differently than they ever realized, which could have significantly altered the outcome.

Behavior chains and the logs necessary for completing them can be tedious work, so many people with intense emotions do not put forth the effort. Research has shown, though, that people who take time to analyze, in specific detail, the events surrounding their destructive behavior recover much more quickly than people who don't. **The sooner you can identify your patterns, the quicker you can begin to develop alternative strategies to deal with your episodes more effectively – so as not to hurt yourself or the ones you care about.**

Copyright 2016 © Jeff Riggenbach, *The Borderline Personality Disorder Toolbox*. All rights reserved.

Cognitive behavior chain analysis can help you have fewer episodes and behave more effectively when you do have them:

1. See it coming.

The sooner you can recognize it is coming, the more precautions you can take.

2. Call a member of your support team.

Remember: call before you decide to hurt yourself. If you have already decided to do something to yourself, that is not the time to call. Call before you have made the decision to act destructively. The earlier you call, the more open you will be to constructive feedback and you may be more easily distracted. Seeking support from friends can be the most important thing in minimizing or refraining from damage in an episode.

3. Use your skills.

If you have been in skills training for a while, you probably have the skills you need to help weather the storm. It is just a matter of grounding yourself and remaining calm enough to remember what the skills are and how to implement them. Remember, you probably have what you need in order to avoid the damage. It can be helpful to write down frequently-used skills on paper and have them in an accessible place for easy access when you sense an episode coming. Revisit soothing, distracting, challenging, coping, being present in the moment, reaching out, etc.. . .

4. Remove yourself from the situation.

The sooner you remove yourself from whatever situation you are in, the more likely you are to avoid or minimize the damage. Get out of that place. Surround yourself with support. Go to a place where you are less likely to do something harmful, even if only to avoid embarrassment.

5. Do something different.

The one sure way to ensure that you will do something hurtful is to stay in the same place, thinking the same thoughts, feeling the same feelings, and doing the same thing. As simple as it may seem, doing something different – anything at all – gives you a better chance of breaking the cycle and not ending up in a bad place.

Copyright 2016 © Jeff Riggenbach, *The Borderline Personality Disorder Toolbox*. All rights reserved.

Balanced Life

Living a balanced lifestyle is important for all humans, but individuals with BPD can especially struggle in this area. While balance is a vital ingredient of stress management for anyone, it is especially important for people who have difficulty regulating their emotions. **Balance can be a stabilizing force in otherwise overwhelming circumstances and emotions.** The following life satisfaction scale uses the PHYSICAL - EMOTIONAL - RELATIONAL - SPIRITUAL model of stress management to assess areas that may be important for you to address.

Place a number from 0 to 10 on the line next to each item below.

0 - means the worst I have ever been
10 - means the best I have ever been.

Marriage/romantic relationship _____

Mental/emotional health _____

Career/employment _____

Recreation/hobbies _____

Spiritual life _____

Physical health _____

Friendships/social life _____

Physical environment (home, cars, etc.) _____

Church/religious participation _____

Extended family _____

Relationship with children (list each separately)

_____ _____

_____ _____

_____ _____

Each aspect of general life satisfaction can be broadly categorized into four areas: **Physical, Emotional, Relational, and Spiritual.** *Self-care* is a term used to describe how well we tend to these four important areas of life. If one or more of these areas is not sufficiently nurtured, we become unbalanced. Living a balanced lifestyle is extremely important for recovery of any kind and will be a point of emphasis in this book. Spend a few minutes to assess yourself in terms of these four areas.

Copyright 2016 © Jeff Riggenbach, *The Borderline Personality Disorder Toolbox*. All rights reserved.

PHYSICAL HEALTH

Am I satisfied with my diet/eating habits? Am I taking vitamins? Eating regular meals? Am I overweight? Underweight? Drinking enough water? Binge eating? Purging? These are common issues for people with BPD. Use this tool to consider possible changes that can be made.

Changes I may need to consider in my overall health could be:

_____

_____

_____

_____

Am I getting regular sleep? Do I have trouble falling asleep? Staying asleep? Am I doing things before I go to bed that are helping me? Hurting me? Am I taking medications properly? Do I have a consistent bedtime routine?

Changes I may need to consider for my sleep habits could be:

_____

_____

_____

_____

Am I satisfied with my physical exercise?

Changes I can make in this area:

_____

_____

_____

_____

Copyright 2016 © Jeff Riggenbach, *The Borderline Personality Disorder Toolbox.* All rights reserved.

SLEEP HYGIENE

Proper "sleep hygiene" (attempts to influence sleep through change of habits and environment) and a healthy diet are cornerstones of healthy self-care. Many people with BPD believe that the only tool for combating sleep difficulties is medication. Sometimes pharmacologic interventions are necessary to address certain sleep-related concerns. However, sleep difficulties often respond to a variety of environmental interventions. **Review the following sleep hygiene guidelines and consider changes you may like to make in these areas:**

Do:

- Monitor room temperature
- Go to bed at the same time daily
- Get up at same time daily
- Use bed for only sleep and sex
- Keep bedroom quiet while sleeping
- Take sleeping meds *as prescribed*
- Establish bedtime routine
- Go to bed when you are tired

Don't:

- Use alcohol or drugs not prescribed for you by a doctor to sleep
- Eat heavily before bed
- Participate in overly stimulating activity before bed
- Drink caffeine/eat sugars close to bedtime
- Watch graphic movies or morbid TV shows close to bedtime
- Take another person's sleeping pills
- Lie in bed for hours if you can't sleep

Copyright 2016 © Jeff Riggenbach, *The Borderline Personality Disorder Toolbox*. All rights reserved.

DIET & NUTRITION

Nutritional neuroscience is a cutting-edge field that looks at the relationship between what we eat and how our brain operates. This issue is not unique to people with BPD. Most Americans underestimate the importance of what food we put in our mouth and how it affects our daily functioning. Here are a few tips for healthy eating:

Healthy eating is:

- Eating what you enjoy
- Eating when you are hungry
- Eating what sustains you
- Eating reasonable portions
- Eating regularly

Unhealthy eating is:

- Skipping meals
- Binge eating
- Eating only sweets
- Overeating when angry/hurt
- Eating too much
- Eating too little

Results of unhealthy eating:

- Obesity
- Type 2 diabetes
- Anorexia
- Bulimia
- Anemia
- Social isolation
- Low self-esteem
- Self-hatred

Unhealthy eating habits often can be traced back to distorted thoughts about food. Examine the list below and identify the distortions about food that you may have:

- *"I live to eat."*
- *"I have to have this food now."*
- *"Food is bad for me."*
- *"If I eat, I am a bad person."*

Copyright 2016 © Jeff Riggenbach, *The Borderline Personality Disorder Toolbox*. All rights reserved.

- *"Food means being out of control."*
- *"Food is necessary for socialization."*
- *"Food is necessary for celebration."*
- *"Eating is wrong."*
- *"Eating protects me/helps me feel secure."*
- *"Food equals weakness."*
- *"If I don't look like _____, I am a failure/undesirable."*

Five changes related to eating/thinking about food that I can make are:

1. _____

   _____

2. _____

   _____

3. _____

   _____

4. _____

   _____

5. _____

   _____

Copyright 2016 © Jeff Riggenbach, *The Borderline Personality Disorder Toolbox*. All rights reserved.

EMOTIONAL HEALTH

BPD is inherently an emotion regulation disorder. Intense emotions are a large part of what is problematic. Destructive behaviors often occur as a means to cope with or regulate intense emotions, not to mention that strong emotions are uncomfortable for the BPD individual as well as people around them.

While sometimes "life just happens," there are other times we can be proactive about what we will do, who we will spend our time with, and where we choose to be. As we plan out our days and weeks, often we have an idea of how being around certain people and places will make us feel. This can also help decrease impulsivity. Use the following tool on emotional health in an attempt to be intentional about this area this week.

What negative emotions will I most likely experience this week?

_____

Am I satisfied with how I deal with those emotions?

_____

What methods have I tried to manage my emotions that have *not* worked?

_____

What techniques have I tried that have worked?

_____

Am I satisfied with how I spend my time?

_____

Am I doing my therapy homework? Am I journaling?

_____

Am I satisfied with my hobbies/interests?

_____

Changes I may need to consider in this area are:

_____

Copyright 2016 © Jeff Riggenbach, *The Borderline Personality Disorder Toolbox*. All rights reserved.

Relational Health

The BPD mood swing is always environmentally triggered and very often specifically relationally triggered. Think about your recent "episodes." How many of them had to do with something somebody said? Didn't say? How someone treated you? Use the following tool to help you anticipate and cope with relational triggers in the upcoming week.

If conflict arises this week with another person, that person is likely to be:

_____

_____

The person I am in conflict with most often is:

_____

_____

The person in my life I have the most difficult time standing up to is:

_____

_____

The person in my life I sometimes treat poorly but wish I didn't is:

_____

_____

Am I generally satisfied with the relationships I have in my life?

_____

_____

If I were to meet new friends who share common interests and values, three places I could potentially meet them are:

_____

_____

Copyright 2016 © Jeff Riggenbach, *The Borderline Personality Disorder Toolbox*. All rights reserved.

One change I could make to improve a relationship today is:

_____

_____

Changes I may need to consider in this area are:

_____

_____

Copyright 2016 © Jeff Riggenbach, *The Borderline Personality Disorder Toolbox*. All rights reserved.

SPIRITUAL HEALTH

Individuals with BPD, probably due to identity issues, often have difficulty with spirituality and having a relationship with God. Some will identify with many different religions or have a variety of spiritual practices throughout their lives, often from very different sources. Explore where you are in this area, to identify opportunities for growth.

To me, God is:

_____

_____

I incorporate my faith into my life in the following way(s):

_____

_____

Spiritual practices, disciplines, and exercises in which I engage regularly are:

_____

_____

Questions I have about my faith are:

_____

_____

One reason I could benefit from growing in my faith is:

_____

_____

One reason I have not made my faith a greater priority in my life is:

_____

_____

My faith can serve as a resource in my recovery in the following ways:

_____

_____

Copyright 2016 © Jeff Riggenbach, *The Borderline Personality Disorder Toolbox*. All rights reserved.

Five changes I could make to enhance my spiritual growth are:

1. _____

2. _____

3. _____

4. _____

5. _____

Copyright 2016 © Jeff Riggenbach, *The Borderline Personality Disorder Toolbox*. All rights reserved.

Finding Identity

Finding identity is a lifetime struggle for some with Borderline Personality Disorder. It is not an exercise you can do once or twice and be done. This requires ongoing and *intentional* work. Use the following tool to help you devise a strategy to develop identity.

One of the diagnostic criteria of BPD is "identity disturbance." Many people wrestle with the issue of identity in different ways. While this may look or feel different to various people, individuals with BPD often say, "I just don't know who I am." This may take various forms, including difficulty establishing hobbies, choosing a major, establishing an occupation, or confusion regarding sexual preference, just to name a few. Also, many people with BPD have become so accustomed to being who everyone else wants them to be, they lose or never establish who they are. **Finding identity can go a long way in helping patients with BPD to establish self-esteem, purpose, and stability in life.** While this is certainly not attainable in a single session, and often continues to develop over a lifetime, searching for areas in which you can find identity may prove to be a worthwhile endeavor, and everyone starts somewhere!

Finding identity starts with answering the question: ***"How do I define myself?"***

Some define themselves by virtue of their relationship to other people. Others do it through an affiliation with a religious group, a hobby, a group of people, by their occupation, or by a particular talent or interest they have. You have probably heard the description of someone "wearing a lot of hats." Consider for a few minutes the "hats" you wear. In doing work to develop identity, it can be helpful to think in terms of *I am, I have, I can,* and *I like*.

For instance,

I am. . . caring, loving, sensitive.

I have. . . a good family.

I can. . . knit/play golf

I like. . . cooking.

Now, in your own words:

I am _____

I have _____

I can _____

I like _____

Copyright 2016 © Jeff Riggenbach, *The Borderline Personality Disorder Toolbox*. All rights reserved.

Near each hat in the following illustration, put one of the ways you currently define yourself or a way that you may like to see yourself in the future. For instance, one particular participant's "hats" included being a *"niece, a sister, a friend, a Christian, a church member, a stamp collector, a chef, a taxi cab driver, a secretary, and a movie goer,"* etc.

Adapted from Velasquez, Maurer, Crouch, and DiClemente, 2001

The "hat" I most identify with is _____

The one I least identify with is _____

Three ways I can develop my identity as a _____ **are:**

1. _____

2. _____

3. _____

Copyright 2016 © Jeff Riggenbach, *The Borderline Personality Disorder Toolbox*. All rights reserved.

GET A LIFE!

Developing a life worth living not only involves **eliminating negative** aspects of life, but also **adding positive** elements to life.

Researchers in Canada discovered that people with BPD do better when they have *part time jobs* or volunteer work of some kind to be involved in. First, this gives people something productive to do with their time. Too much time on our hands to dwell on negatives is not good for anyone.

Secondly, this can build self-esteem. It can be a chance to work on developing some mastery: a chance to get good at something and feel accomplished. It can be an opportunity to help others. It can contribute to your income. It can be an opportunity to support a cause you believe in or do something you think is important in the world. Adding positive value to your life does not always have to include employment. While work is often helpful, hobbies, interests or other things you listed in your Finding Identity tool can be incorporated here. Use the area below to list some ways you might "get a life."

Getting a Life!

1._____

_____

2._____

_____

3._____

_____

4._____

_____

5._____

_____

Copyright 2016 © Jeff Riggenbach, *The Borderline Personality Disorder Toolbox*. All rights reserved.

LIVING PURPOSEFULLY

When I ask clients what they have going on the next week, I often hear people with BPD say things like, "Well it depends what happens." It is as if *what they will do* is totally dependent upon others.

It is true that *occasionally* we have to react to people and situations in our environment, but *we have control* over a lot of what we do. How we *choose* to spend our time is largely up to us.

People who live life more intentionally find more happiness, meaning, and contentment in their lives, because they are living for a purpose, rather than just reacting to situations around them. While it may seem tedious, intentionally planning how you will spend your days can be of tremendous benefit. Use the following scheduling tool to be more intentional about your living.

Daily Activity Log		
Date / /	Planned Activity	Actual Activity
Midnight		
1:00 am		
2:00 am		
3:00 am		
4:00 am		
5:00 am		
6:00 am		
7:00 am		
8:00 am		
9:00 am		
10:00 am		
11:00 am		
12:00 pm		
1:00 pm		
2:00 pm		
3:00 pm		
4:00 pm		
5:00 pm		
6:00 pm		
7:00 pm		
8:00 pm		
9:00 pm		
10:00 pm		
11:00 pm		

Copyright 2016 © Jeff Riggenbach, *The Borderline Personality Disorder Toolbox*. All rights reserved.

MONITORING MY PROGRESS

Hopefully, at this point, you are well on your way to recovery. Yes, ON YOUR WAY – recovery is a lifelong process. You (or anyone else, for that matter) will continue to make choices and use your skills in ways that shape your life – some for the better, some for the worse. It does not mean you won't make wrong choices. It does not mean you will absolutely never have a relapse. And it certainly doesn't mean life will be smooth sailing up the mountain. **Life will continue to change, and you will continue to need to adapt.** But, hopefully, you have learned the skills necessary to traverse the terrain that awaits you.

It is important to understand a common myth related to recovery. Some people leave, confident of their progress, and are surprised when the road gets rough. The road to recovery is not a smooth, gradual, continuous upward climb – it still involves rough terrain, ups and downs (as represented by the graphic in the tool below) but it is important to remember where you started and which direction you are headed.

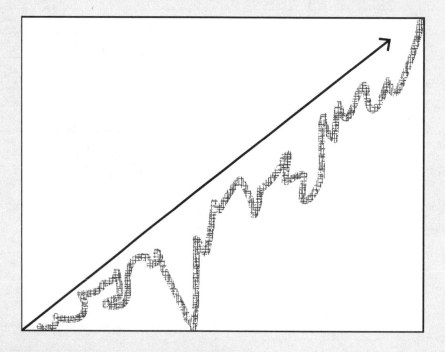

So be prepared for some bad days. Don't beat yourself up when you slip. Hold yourself accountable, but treat yourself with grace. Learn from your mistakes. Seek God and others and use what you have learned, and you will be effective at dealing with whatever your mountain looks like.

Copyright 2016 © Jeff Riggenbach, *The Borderline Personality Disorder Toolbox*. All rights reserved.

Relapse Prevention

As you advance in your learning process, a key challenge to managing your illness becomes understanding the skills you have – *when* to use them and *how* to use them, rather than developing new skills.

A good majority of relapses occur when people, who have all of the skills necessary to manage their condition, don't implement them correctly, and they relapse. A relapse can be defined as reverting back to any undesired behavior targeted for change. In an oversimplified sense, **relapse prevention involves developing healthy habits in place of unhealthy habits. It involves analyzing what you are doing well, and creating ways to continue doing those things effectively.** It also involves gaining an understanding of circumstances around times that you slip back into harmful behaviors, and constructing new and alternative ways to deal with those situations to decrease the likelihood that you will "slip" the next time the urge hits.

First, make a list of things you are doing well to manage your illness now; then develop relapse prevention plans.

Things I'm Doing Right!!

1. _____

2. _____

3. _____

4. _____

5. _____

6. _____

7. _____

8. _____

9. _____

10. _____

Copyright 2016 © Jeff Riggenbach, *The Borderline Personality Disorder Toolbox*. All rights reserved.

Steps For Relapse Prevention

Analyze the situation in which you relapsed. What was the trigger?

_____

_____

Do a behavior chain analysis. At what points (links) could you have done something differently?

_____

_____

Develop a list of skills you didn't use in this scenario that you could try next time.

_____

_____

Walk through the incident step-by-step and at each point ask, "What could I have done differently?" From your list, choose 3 things you could have done differently at EACH point.

_____

_____

_____

Don't beat yourself up. Take responsibility, but forgive yourself, let it go, and move on!

CHAPTER 7

CRISIS MANAGEMENT TOOLS

All people are more likely to act erratically when emotions are running high. One of the challenges for individuals with BPD is that emotions are running high so much more often than for other people.

Having a set of tools specifically designed for dealing with crises is a very important part of any recovery plan for people with BPD. Some of these tools are designed to help you avert crises before they hit. Others can be implemented in times of crisis to minimize the damage.

GROUNDING

Grounding techniques are a set of tools that can help people with BPD to detach from emotional pain. **When overwhelmed with emotional intensity, you need a way to detach so that you can gain control over your feelings and stay safe.** As long as you are grounding, it is very unlikely you will act on those emotions and hurt yourself. Grounding "anchors" you to the present and to reality. Consider which of the following principles and strategies related to grounding may be helpful for you.

- Stay present in the moment
- Keep your eyes open
- Pay attention to your environment
- Focus on the present, not the past
- Describe your surroundings in detail
- Focus on all five senses (I feel, I hear, I see, I smell, I taste)
- Orient self (my name is…the date is…I am located in…)
- Work your way through the alphabet. Identify a word that starts with each letter.
- Run cool water on your wrist
- Practice stretching exercises

I will try the following grounding tools:

1. _____

2. _____

3. _____

4. _____

5. _____

Copyright 2016 © Jeff Riggenbach, *The Borderline Personality Disorder Toolbox*. All rights reserved.

Episode Management

Marsha Linehan, the developer of DBT, describes the intense episodes many people with BPD experience as "emotional tornadoes." Recommended guidelines for taking precautions from an actual tornado can serve as a helpful guide for weathering the intensity of emotional tornadoes and managing these episodes more effectively.

1. **Identify warning signs.** The first key for staying safe in the face of a possible tornado is to notice the warning signs. Meteorologists have a number of tools at their disposal including Doppler radar to identify atmospheric conditions and potential weather patterns likely to affect a given area. A "watch" warns people in that area that "conditions are favorable for tornadic activity."

   Recommendations for early intervention include developing an emergency preparedness kit, purchasing a specialized weather radio, and, if you live in an area that is especially vulnerable to tornadoes, purchasing a safe room.

2. **Triggers** (know when a tornado has touched down in your area) are things that happen or said that instigate or "set off" an episode. Identifying patterns can be helpful in dealing with episodes before they happen or at least before they get out of control.

3. **Take precautions.** When a real tornado has touched down in your area, the National Weather Service recommends a variety of measures that you can take to protect yourself.

   Similarly, there is a model for individuals with borderline personality disorder to use to manage "emotional" tornados:

What are my warning signs?

- What in my life makes "conditions favorable" for me to have an episode?
- When am I most vulnerable?
- Are there people who wear me down?
- Are there people who influence me to make bad decisions?
- Am I more vulnerable when I am hungry? Angry? Lonely? Tired?

What are my triggers?

- What types of situations set me off?
- What kinds of comments set me off?
- What people tend to make those comments?
- Are there themes in topics that seem to trigger me?
- Are there smells that trigger me?
- Are there songs that evoke strong emotions?

What precautions could I take?

- Are there people I need to avoid completely?

Copyright 2016 © Jeff Riggenbach, *The Borderline Personality Disorder Toolbox*. All rights reserved.

- If I can't avoid them completely, are there others I can have around me as buffers when I am around the people I can't avoid?
- Do I need to rearrange my schedule in some way?
- What can I do differently to ensure that I get more sleep?
- Do I need to make changes in my eating habits?
- What can I do to be less lonely?
- What can I do to tolerate loneliness better?
- Have I been surrounding myself with positive people?
- Am I spiritually where I want to be?

My Episode Management Plan Includes:

Copyright 2016 © Jeff Riggenbach, *The Borderline Personality Disorder Toolbox*. All rights reserved.

REASONS FOR LIVING

Having reasons for living is important for all humans, but it is especially so for those who struggle with recurring suicidal thoughts. A number of "reasons for living" inventories have been developed and are available in the public domain. The following is a modified version. **Use the following to identify reasons that it is important for you to continue to live.** It is often helpful to have these easily accessible when thoughts of suicide or self-injury recur.

1. I believe that I have a responsibility to my family.
2. I believe only God has the right to take a life.
3. I am afraid of death.
4. I do not yet believe things are bad enough that I would rather be dead.
5. It is against my religious beliefs to kill myself.
6. I believe I still have something to offer the world.
7. I want to see my children grow up and be there to support them.
8. I still have things I want to accomplish in life.
9. I am afraid of the unknown.
10. There is no evidence that, if I die, I will be in a better place.
11. No matter how badly I feel now, I know it will not last.
12. I believe life is too sacred to end it.
13. I want to experience joy again.
14. I am afraid it will not work and I'll become a vegetable.
15. I am afraid of going to Hell.
16. I believe committing suicide would damage my children psychologically.
17. I am afraid of the pain.
18. I would not want my family to feel guilty afterwards.
19. I do not want people to think I was selfish.
20. I still have a desire to live.

Below, list your reasons for living. They can be directly from this list, related to this list, or completely different reasons.

My Reasons For Living

1. _____

2. _____

3. _____

4. _____

5. _____

Copyright 2016 © Jeff Riggenbach, *The Borderline Personality Disorder Toolbox*. All rights reserved.

SAFEGUARD THE ENVIRONMENT

Safeguarding the environment is a tool designed for you to **separate yourself from the means of acting on your harmful urges**. For instance, if your urge is to cut yourself, safeguarding may involve removing any sharp things from the house. If your urge is to overdose on medication, safeguarding may involve allowing a loved one to lock up your medication and dispense it to you. If your urge involves use of alcohol, safeguarding may involve removing all alcohol from the house. If your urge involves spending money impulsively that you don't have, safeguarding may involve giving your credit card to your spouse until your urge subsides.

We have a patient in our program who struggles with urges to self-injure. Although she has gradually been willing to get rid of the "kit" she has used to harm herself, she refuses to get rid of her final blade. Her safeguarding at this point involves putting her blade in a glass of ice and freezing it. She still has it, but if she chooses to act on her urge to self-harm, she will have to wait until it thaws. Safeguarding does not guarantee you will not act destructively; it merely delays action, giving you time to think more rationally and change your mind.

SAFEGUARDING YOUR ENVIRONMENT

Temptation Behavior	Steps I will Take to Safeguard
Cut	1. Get rid of all blades 2. Leave my house so I won't be around other sharp objects that would tempt me 3. Take my son with me – hurting myself is not an option when I am with him
Go To The Casino	1. Give my cards and all cash to my husband so I don't have access 2. Spend the weekend with my aunt where there are no casinos

Temptation Behavior	Steps I will Take to Safeguard

Copyright 2016 © Jeff Riggenbach, *The Borderline Personality Disorder Toolbox*. All rights reserved.

SAFETY PLANNING

Once you have identified your reasons for living and have safeguarded your environment, it is important to commit to a personal safety plan. Anyone in treatment for borderline personality disorder should always have a safety plan. **It is important to know your plan, have copies of your plan, and have at least one other person who knows your plan and can assist you in implementing it in case that destructive urges recur.**

A safety plan is not a simple "yes" or "no," I promise I will be safe. It is much more specific and proactive. It requires that you identify several specific things you promise to do if you have a dangerous urge come over you, rather than acting on that urge. Use the following tool to develop your personal safety plan.

My Safety Plan

I, _____, contract for my safety. This means I promise not to act on my thoughts of attempting to commit suicide. Before acting on my urges to harm or kill myself, I agree to:

1. _____

2. _____

3. _____

4. _____

5. _____

Copyright 2016 © Jeff Riggenbach, *The Borderline Personality Disorder Toolbox*. All rights reserved.

CHAPTER 8

RELATIONAL TOOLS

Relationships often prove difficult for people with BPD. Most desperately want meaningful relationships. But misunderstandings and hard feelings often make healthy relationships elusive. Some people become so hardened by failed relationships that they become desensitized and quit trying. Others fear another abandonment so strongly that, in order to avoid another rejection experience, they choose to not have anyone in their lives. The following relational tools are designed to enhance this part of your recovery.

BUILDING RELATIONSHIPS: TAKE A TEST DRIVE

Interpersonal relationships can be very problematic for those with BPD. Most people with intense emotions *desperately* feel they need relationships. Many with BPD, or other relational disorders, often attempt to develop relationships very quickly, and tend to place intimacy and trust in relationships sooner than is wise, considering how little they really know the person. Many, then, get hurt in relationships, and eventually have been hurt so many times that trusting again is difficult.

Some people with these issues put up walls that keep people from getting in. These walls work in the sense that they keep people from getting in to hurt them; however, they keep people from getting in to help them as well. Others never put up these walls, and continue to seek relationships, but do so with unhealthy people. **Relationships are important to everybody. The reality is that people need people.**

Since relationships are so crucial, especially for people who struggle with regulating emotions, establishing healthy relationships is an important part of recovery. Sometimes we encourage people to take relationships for a "test drive" similar to how they might drive a car, in order to see what they like and what they don't like before they decide which people get to stay permanently in their relationship "circles."

Take a few minutes to examine the relationships you have, writing them in the circles in a place that shows how close you consider them to be.

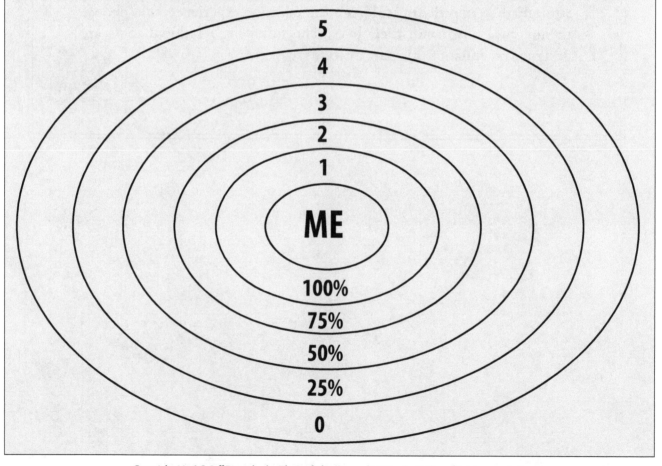

Copyright 2016 © Jeff Riggenbach, *The Borderline Personality Disorder Toolbox*. All rights reserved.

Building My Support Team

Research shows that a person's support system plays a crucial role in how well they are able to recover from Borderline Personality Disorder. **While evaluating the people in your circles can have many benefits, one obvious benefit has to do with using them to build your support system.**

Some will find they already have enough supportive people in their circles one and two. Some will note that they may not have the people they desire in circles one and two, but that they may have people in circles 3, 4, or 5 who may be candidates to move in closer over time. Others identify that they have nobody currently in their circles trustworthy enough to have on their support team, so they need to identify other places they can go to meet supportive people (a later tool).

While it is important to have people you trust and can share anything with on your support team, many people also have people on their teams they may not share personal stuff with, but who they can call just to go to a movie or a sporting event or have some fun with (even if it is more of a superficial relationship). These relationships can have value as well.

Use the following tool to identify people you can reach out to for different reasons and add to your support team.

My Support Team

	<u>Name</u>	<u>Phone Number</u>
1.	_____	_____
2.	_____	_____
3.	_____	_____
4.	_____	_____
5.	_____	_____
6.	_____	_____
7.	_____	_____
8.	_____	_____
9.	_____	_____
10.	_____	_____

Copyright 2016 © Jeff Riggenbach, *The Borderline Personality Disorder Toolbox*. All rights reserved.

STABILIZING MY CIRCLES: "I HATE YOU; DON'T LEAVE ME."

While taking your relationship for a "test drive," consider these questions that may help you examine what changes you may want to make to your circles (see page 150). Use this tool to help stabilize your relationships and end your "I hate you; don't leave me" pattern.

What changes would you like to make to your circles?

_____

_____

Who are the people you would like to have closer in? Further out?

_____

_____

Some hurtful things I have done in the past that have damaged one or more relationships:

_____

_____

Some helpful things I have done in the past that have been helped me in maintaining relationships:

_____

_____

Changes I could make in the way I relate to people may include:

_____

Would you like to add people to your circles who currently aren't there?

_____

What type of people would you like to add?

_____

Where might you go to meet people like that?

_____

One step I am willing to take today to start work on my circles is:

_____

Copyright 2016 © Jeff Riggenbach, *The Borderline Personality Disorder Toolbox*. All rights reserved.

SETTING BOUNDARIES

The boundaries we set with one another determine how we allow people in our circles. They determine how close we are emotionally to others. They help determine how we allow people to treat us and, thereby, what we experience in our relationships.

Many people with BPD grew up in chaotic families where boundaries were not respected or modeled. If you grew up in such a family, you may have a difficult time setting boundaries that enable you to feel safe in relationships and not be taken advantage of. You also may struggle not to violate others' boundaries.

Developing and maintaining healthy boundaries is essential for those learning to manage relationships while dealing with intense emotions. Healthy boundaries will not only help you feel more safe and secure in the relationships you are in, they will also help the other people you care about feel more secure and less threatened in the relationship as well.

People Who Have Healthy Boundaries:
- Interact with people effectively
- Frequently get what they want in relationships
- Know what they will and will not do
- Know what they will and will not allow others to do
- Can set limits and still love
- Do not violate the personal space of others
- Do not take on the responsibilities of others
- Can be responsible *to* others without feeling responsible *for* them
- Feel safe and secure
- Have healthy "circles"

People Who Have Unhealthy Boundaries:
- Frequently have difficulty in relationships
- Have difficulty getting their needs met in relationships
- Trust too easily and share too much personal information with the wrong people
- Trust too little and don't have people with whom they can open up
- Violate the personal space of others
- Ask inappropriate personal questions of people they don't know well
- Feel responsible for other people's behavior and feelings
- Often live lives driven by guilt
- Choose actions based upon what will please others rather than based upon their convictions
- Tolerate unhealthy or inappropriate behaviors from others
- Feel unsafe in relationships
- Have unhealthy "circles"

Three people in my life I have boundary difficulties with are:

_____

_____

_____

_____

One boundary I will set this week is:

_____

_____

_____

_____

Copyright 2016 © Jeff Riggenbach, _The Borderline Personality Disorder Toolbox_. All rights reserved.

CHAPTER 9

SCHEMA FOCUSED TOOLS

Schema Focused Therapy has been shown to be a new and effective treatment for BPD. Although it is not as widely known (in the United States anyway - it is the treatment of choice in some countries) as some of the other treatments, SFT has some valuable tools to offer to the person with BPD.

Because true "purist" schema therapy places a high degree of emphasis on the therapeutic relationship between the client and the professional, no set of "tools" can do justice to what the actual treatment experience would be like. But here are a few of the concepts related to getting at deeper level beliefs (schemas) that drive behaviors.

Get a Filter Change:
Identifying Core Beliefs

Schemas, or core beliefs, serve as filters through which we process information as we experience events in life.

According to Aaron Beck, the founder of cognitive therapy, we all have core beliefs in three areas: beliefs about ourselves, beliefs about others, and beliefs about the world in general. Judith Beck, at the Beck Institute for Cognitive Therapy, helps patients visualize core beliefs in the following way that resembles a "Pac-Man" figure:

One of the characteristics of people with BPD is distorted beliefs in any or all of these three areas. For example, some people may have a core belief about themselves such as:

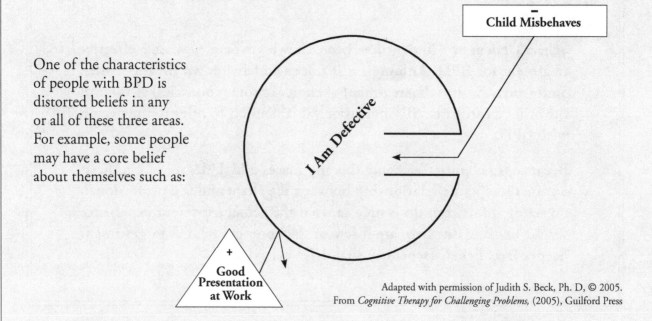

Adapted with permission of Judith S. Beck, Ph. D, © 2005. From *Cognitive Therapy for Challenging Problems*, (2005), Guilford Press

Depending upon the content of the belief, certain things "fit" and are received well by the individual. Contradictory messages do not "fit" and are often met with resistance. For example, people who have the core belief, "I am defective," receive/hear/believe some things better than others. For instance, with this core belief, one may not believe that she made a good presentation at work, even though 30 people may have told her so. On the contrary, if her child misbehaves that day, that "evidence" will be more easily "heard" to support her belief.

Take a few minutes to examine your core beliefs in each life area. Remember, these will play an important role in how you filter information and are thereby able to communicate with others in your life. Several possible core beliefs in each area are provided on the following pages. If you believe that one of these characterizes your core belief in that area adequately, feel free to use it. If not, you may use your own words to describe your beliefs in the three areas.

Copyright 2016 © Jeff Riggenbach, *The Borderline Personality Disorder Toolbox*. All rights reserved.

Write your core beliefs in the circle by each area of life listed:

Core Beliefs about Myself

"I am generally a good person and am worthy of love."
"I am vulnerable/unsafe."
"I am incompetent (can't do anything right)."
"I am unlovable."
"I am worthless/defective (damaged goods)."
"I have to have it now/can't show self-control."

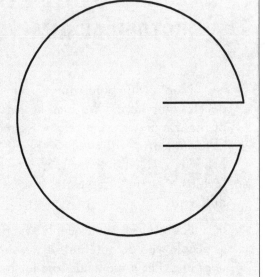

Core Beliefs about Others

"Others are basically good."
"Others are untrustworthy."
"Other people are generally bad and
deserve to be punished."
"Others will leave me."
"Others basically have good intentions,
but are unreliable."

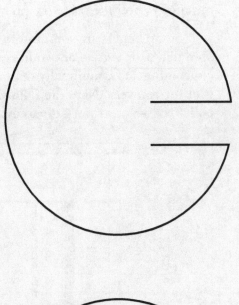

Core Beliefs about the World

"The world is basically dangerous and
life is unfair."
"The world is basically good and life is
generally fair."

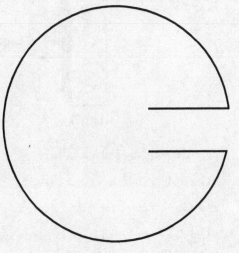

Copyright 2016 © Jeff Riggenbach, *The Borderline Personality Disorder Toolbox*. All rights reserved.

"What are the legs to my table?"
Historical Analysis of Development of Beliefs

People with Borderline Personality Disorder often wonder, "Where in the world did these beliefs come from?" We stress to patients that this is an excellent question, as nobody comes out of the womb with core beliefs! Exercises can be done to discover what exactly contributed to the development of these beliefs. Leslie Sokol, a faculty member at the Beck Institute, compares a belief to a tabletop. In the same way that tabletops need legs to hold them up, beliefs need legs or "evidence" to support them. *"Evidence"* is in quotation marks because different people *count* evidence differently.

For instance, some people who believe in aliens may have heard the same stories (information) as people who do not, but for various reasons, one person "counts" it as "evidence" and the other does not. The same holds true for beliefs about ourselves. Anyone who has a failure belief about themselves, whether they realize it or not, has collected "evidence" that they have assigned specific meaning to over the years to support that belief.

Some beliefs are common to all people with BPD (abandonment); other beliefs may be seen in a wide variety of conditions (unlovable/failure). This exercise can be a little more time consuming and emotionally draining than some of the previous tools, but it can be a powerful tool for recovery. Note the following example for a "failure" belief. Then identify your own belief you want to work on accompanied by your "legs" (supporting evidence).

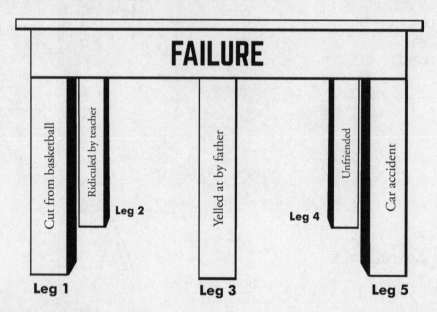

Evidence that I am a failure:

Leg 1: Cut from 8th grade basketball team

Leg 2: Ridiculed for science project by teacher

Leg 3: Father yelled at me in garage for mistake on construction project

Leg 4: Unfriended by classmate

Leg 5: Got into a car accident while texting and driving

Copyright 2016 © Jeff Riggenbach, *The Borderline Personality Disorder Toolbox*. All rights reserved.

The following questions may be helpful in reflecting back on different periods of your life to uncover some of the experiences you counted as evidence to support your beliefs (legs to hold up your table). Note this example is from my previously published *CBT Toolbox* of "evidence" one individual counted to support his belief that he was a failure. Then use your answers from these questions to identify your own "legs" (evidence) to support your "table" (belief you identified). You may need assistance from your therapist to get the most out of this tool.

The first time I ever remember feeling _____[identify as a

belief] **was** _____

Things in my life that influenced me to feel that way were:

Family members

_____

Friends/Peers

_____

Other significant people

_____

Experiences during my elementary school years

_____

Experiences during my junior high years

_____

Experiences during my high school years

_____

Experiences during my college/young adult years

_____

Significant experiences since then

_____

Copyright 2016 © Jeff Riggenbach, *The Borderline Personality Disorder Toolbox*. All rights reserved.

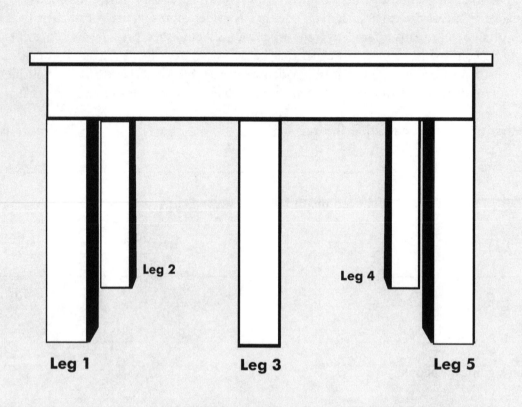

Evidence that I am a_____**:**

Leg 1 _____

Leg 2 _____

Leg 3 _____

Leg 4 _____

Leg 5 _____

Copyright 2016 © Jeff Riggenbach, *The Borderline Personality Disorder Toolbox*. All rights reserved.

DESENSITIZE YOUR BUTTONS!
USING EVIDENCE LOGS TO DECREASE YOUR REACTIVITY

Developing skills to manage symptoms of BPD is of course helpful. But eventually, wouldn't it be nice to get to the place where you aren't as reactive in the first place?

Changing beliefs can help accelerate this process. Beliefs mean different things to different people. For instance, people who are working from the unhealthy belief that they are failures have specific ideas as to what that means. Perhaps the opposite healthy belief they are working to build is that they can succeed. **People count *accomplishments* differently from *successes* because different things are important to different people.** Success may be evident as:

- Good grades
- A strong attendance record
- Keeping the house clean
- Work-related projects
- Scientific exploration/advancement
- Promotions

- Salary
- Saving money
- Successful children
- Completing a task
- Finishing a daily "to-do" list
- Cleaning something

As you can see, the *components* of the belief of *success* are different to different people. To build healthy beliefs, it is important to identify the *components* of your healthy belief.

My Belief Components

1. _____

2. _____

3. _____

Ongoing evidence logs are another important tool for developing more healthy beliefs and becoming less reactive. While previous tools have asked you to review your life and look for "evidence" from the past, ongoing evidence logs ask you to be mindful of evidence in your everyday life.

Since your unhealthy filters will naturally be pointing you toward negative evidence, it is often necessary to purposefully seek out positive evidence. *Purposefully seek out* doesn't mean "make it up" if it legitimately isn't there, but rather it means to try to pay attention to any evidence that legitimately may be present yet missed due to your negative filter. **It is helpful to collect evidence for each belief you struggle with, but it is recommended to pick only one or two to focus on at a given time.**

Evidence that I can succeed

Date	Evidence
3/12	Passed Test
3/13	Received compliment
3/16	Got monthly bills paid
3/20	Completed errands
3/22	Interviewed for a job

I *CAN* SUCCEED

Evidence that I can be _____ (healthy belief) log

Date	Evidence

Copyright 2016 © Jeff Riggenbach, *The Borderline Personality Disorder Toolbox*. All rights reserved.

PRACTICAL APPLICATION SUMMARY

Personal growth is hard work. In an attempt to take in all the information you can, it is easy to lose "the forest for the trees." Use this final tool to record major learning points. What are the most helpful principles you have learned in this book? What are the most practical? What action steps will you take immediately to further your recovery?

Things I've Learned

1. _____

2. _____

3. _____

4. _____

5. _____

6. _____

7. _____

8. _____

9. _____

10. _____

My Action Plan:

_____

_____

_____

_____

_____

_____

_____

Copyright 2016 © Jeff Riggenbach, *The Borderline Personality Disorder Toolbox*. All rights reserved.

CHAPTER 10

MEDICATION & HOSPITALIZATION TOOLS

Whether or not to take medications is always a decision to be made in conjunction with your psychiatrist.

Medications

No medication has been approved for the treatment of Borderline Personality Disorder or the symptoms of BPD. Why are so many people with BPD on multiple medications then?

Excellent question! Perhaps for a few reasons. **The first is because 90% of people diagnosed with BPD also meet criteria for at least one other condition that does respond to medication.** For example, a person diagnosed with BPD may also have what is now called persistent depressive disorder. While antidepressants won't help you feel less "depressed" when someone says something hurtful to you, it can help if, in addition to being interpersonally reactive, you also struggle with low energy, difficulty getting out of bed for weeks at a time, and lack of interest in activities. Thus medications can be helpful for treating conditions that are not part of the BPD but frequently accompany the BPD.

The second reason is that, even though medications don't "treat" BPD in the same way that they do bipolar disorder, for example, for some can be helpful for managing its symptoms. BPD manifests in different ways in different people at different times. BPD can manifest itself with panic attacks, episodes of rage, mood swings and many other presentations.

Although therapy is primary and medication is secondary for treating BPD, some medications can be useful for managing symptoms. Unfortunately, many people with BPD don't realize this, and many mental health practitioners do a poor job of explaining this to their patients.

So, many patients believe taking medications will treat their condition without therapy, resulting in a couple of unintended consequences. One consequence is that individuals with BPD keep trying new meds waiting for "the right medication for me" and thinking, "As soon as I get the right combination of meds, I'll be OK." It is a common experience for many people with BPD to present for treatment at our BPD program having been on multiple medications over the years and saying, "None of them really worked much." A second consequence is that people may never even seek therapy because they think they just have not found the right combination of medication.

Good general rules of thumb for people with BPD:

1) Be on as few medications as possible

2) Know every medication you are on and why it has been prescribed for you

3) Don't expect medications to "cure" you; know they are just band aids and that the primary treatment for BPD is therapy.

Use the following Medication Tracker to track your medications.

Copyright 2016 © Jeff Riggenbach, *The Borderline Personality Disorder Toolbox*. All rights reserved.

MEDICATION TRACKER

Medication/dosage	Prescriber	Reason	First Prescription	Benefits/Side Effects

Copyright 2016 © Jeff Riggenbach, *The Borderline Personality Disorder Toolbox*. All rights reserved.

HOSPITALIZATION

Hospitalization is your final tool. This is because hospitalization should be your last resort. This is one of the many areas in which people with Borderline Personality Disorder differ.

Some people with BPD hate going in the hospital. If this is you, this needs to be something outlined in your treatment agreement with your therapist. You MUST be willing to go in the hospital if it is necessary to ensure your safety. However, many people with BPD find comfort in going into the hospital. They experience it as a safe place amidst the chaos of their lives. If this is you, it is vital that you hear my next sentence: **Research is clear that the more often people with BPD go into the hospital, the worse their prognosis.**

Nobody knows exactly why this is. One theory that makes sense is that many people with BPD frequently seek *external* solutions to their internal problems. It is common that people with BPD have tried multiple medications, natural remedies, electroshock therapy, EMDR and many other external aids. Hospitalization works similarly. People view the hospital as an opportunity for others to *do something to them* to make them better.

Also seeking shelter from the stresses of their lives gives them a temporary respite. However, when they are discharged, they have the same stresses awaiting them the minute they get out and sometimes problems get worse: work piles up, supervisors are unhappy due to missed time, resentment builds and further damages relationship problems, the rent is further overdue, etc.

A final note on this: If you, or your therapist, believe that hospitalization is necessary, do all you can to make it a *skillful hospitalization* vs. an *unskillful hospitalization.*

Hospitalizations should be short! One to three days is optimal (if no extenuating medical circumstances exist). The goals should be recommitting to a safety plan that works and being discharged quickly to re-engage in outpatient treatment.

Finally, take responsibility for your hospitalization. Be clear about your treatment goals. After all, they are your goals! Work your treatment goals. Use the brief hospitalization to prepare you for your upcoming life that still must be faced. Don't use that time in the hospital as just a vacation from your problems. Use the following tool to guide hospitalization.

HOSPITALIZATION

Some warning signs I might need to go in the hospital are_____

Thoughts, feelings, and behaviors I might experience that are concerning but, with help, I can manage out of the hospital_____

Thoughts, feelings, and behaviors I might experience that would be a sign I DEFINITELY need to be hospitalized to stay safe_____

People in my life I promise to contact if I need to be hospitalized are:

1. _____

2. _____

3. _____

Copyright 2016 © Jeff Riggenbach, *The Borderline Personality Disorder Toolbox*. All rights reserved.

CHAPTER 11
WHAT HEALTH CARE PROFESSIONALS NEED TO KNOW

Perhaps the *most important* thing for professionals to know is that all people with Borderline Personality Disorder are not the same. Layden and Newman at the University of Pennsylvania have identified three different subtypes. And not all people with BPD fit nicely into one of these categories either.

1. **The Avoidant / Dependent Subtype**. These individuals present more like trauma patients in a lot of ways. They often have anxiety, are vigilant and shy. Their presentation is often "shame-based" in nature. They are rarely attention-seeking. If they self-injure (and they may not), they are usually ashamed by it. It is usually well hidden so people won't see or ask about it. Cutting with this subtype may occur on the stomach, feet, or breasts, so it can be easily hidden with clothes or shoes. These individuals desperately want to date, marry, and have friendships, but often are too fearful to initiate or respond. Once in an unhealthy relationship, it is almost impossible for these individuals to leave.

2. **The Narcissistic / Histrionic Subtype**. Extreme manifestations of these individuals represent the stereotype of many "worst case scenarios" often portrayed in the media. This subtype tends to be more attention-seeking, has more difficulty with empathy, and is often highly social/gregarious and sometimes flirtatious or sexualized. This is the subtype that often cuts superficially in visible spots such as horizontally on wrists and often has a motive of eliciting a sympathetic response from others. After they self-injure, or demonstrate verbal or physical aggression towards others, they typically experience an emotional response of guilt, self-hate, or shame. Relational instability and "relationship hopping" is a hallmark quality of this subtype, but it should be known that these individuals usually genuinely want connected relationships with others. Although there is a range within this group of individuals as well, this is the most common subtype.

3. **The Paranoid / Antisocial Subtype**. These individuals often have a "dark" presentation. They self-injure because they have a profound hatred for themselves and the motive is almost always to punish themselves for being "bad" or "evil" people. They don't care if you see it or not. Evidence of self-injury can be found anywhere on their bodies. They aren't trying to hide it from you. But they are not trying to show it off either. These self-injurers' motives have nothing to do with you. They are often less trusting of others than most. Many will claim to "hate people." They can treat themselves or others horribly and have no remorse because they continue to believe the violated party "deserved it." Like all borderline disordered individuals, they have difficulty connecting with others, but unlike the previous subtypes, they often don't want friendships or dating relationships and really would prefer being alone. It is even common for them to have difficulty attaching to their children.

OUTPATIENT CARE

Borderline Personality Disorder should be primarily treated at the outpatient level of care. Although patients with BPD do require hospitalization with more frequency than most populations, the outpatient level of care is the one that will determine how successfully the patient recovers from this condition. As noted earlier, medication can play an adjunctive role, but the primary treatment of BPD is psychotherapy.

Empirically supported modalities, such as Dialectical Behavior Therapy (DBT) and Mentalization-Based Treatment (MBT), were described earlier in this book (see Chapter 1 for a summary). DBT (Linehan, 1991), SFT (Young, 1991), CBT (Freeman, 2004), and MBT (Bateman & Fonagy, 2010) are among the most empirically supported approaches for treating BPD.

Note that the *structure* of these programs is likely at least as valuable as the content. Most major cities have BPD treatment programs of some kind. Evidence-based practice should guide your treatment of BPD. Although evidence-based treatment can be applied somewhat flexibly to best meet the needs of the client, many clinicians have done harm to patients by not being informed about evidence-based treatments for BPD and not including essential ingredients in their therapy.

Not all therapies are appropriate for treating BPD. If you lack sufficient training, get supervision, consultation, or additional training on treatments known to be effective for BPD, or refer your patient to a qualified provider.

SUICIDE AND SELF-INJURY

It should also be noted that 20% - 25% of individuals with BPD will never commit a self-damaging act. Many will have suicidal ideation, but the comparative frequency of suicidal thoughts vs. suicidal or parasuicidal actions is actually quite rare. Having suicidal thinking is NOT grounds for hospitalization. Research is clear that the more we hospital individuals with BPD, the worse their prognosis becomes (Paris, 2010).

HOSPITALIZATION

Hospitalization should be considered a last resort, and should only be defaulted to if a patient is not able to commit to a (clinically believable) safety plan. Even following medical clearance or treatment for self-injury or suicide attempt, if the patient is able to commit to a reasonable safety plan, hospitalization likely is not indicated.

BPD patients can be very different from depressed patients, who are typically more acutely suicidal. Oftentimes, once the BPD individual has done their act, it is over for them. Chapter 2 highlights common functions of this behavior, but unlike traditional Axis I depressed patients, their motivation is not death. And in cases where they don't want to die, once their behavior has served its function, the safety risk decreases in a way that is significantly different from that of depressed individuals. If their motive was to die, and they are still alive, they usually remain at high risk and require hospitalization.

All of this is to say, assess your BPD patients thoroughly and accurately at each stage before making your disposition, to ensure it is the best clinical decision for that particular patient.

If the decision is made to admit the patient, hospitalizations should be: 1) brief and 2) unpleasant. Hospitalizations for the BPD patient should typically be one to three days (excluding any extraneous medication/medical issue that needs to be monitored or other clinically justified exceptions). Goals of hospitalization should be immediate safety, stabilization, and referral back to outpatient treatment. The longer the patient stays in the hospital, the more it is generally associated with deterioration in functioning upon discharge.

Secondly, it is again noteworthy that people with BPD vary in terms of their attitude toward hospitalization. Some hate to be hospitalized. For these individuals, it is important that treatment providers assess to ensure the patient is not simply saying what he/she knows staff wants to hear in order to be discharged.

Outpatient providers are more apt to be required to hospitalize these individuals against their wills when the provider thinks danger to self or others is imminent and being minimized. Others with BPD find comfort in the hospital. Some even continue to make suicidal threats in order NOT to be discharged. With this group of individuals, it is important not to inadvertently reinforce unhealthy messages. Education is vital for staff and BPD individuals. Even though some feel safer in the hospital and experience it as a refuge from the chaos of their lives, it is important that everyone realizes that the longer the patient stays in the hospital, the worse it really is for him/her.

Finally, *unpleasant* simply means hospitalizations should not be a vacation. Patients should work hard while they are there to determine what component of their outpatient plan failed to keep them safe, revise the plan, and return to working it. The worst thing we as professionals can do for this population is to admit patients at the first mention of any threat and pamper them for fourteen days on an inpatient unit. When hospitalizations are absolutely necessary, they should be brief in length and skillful in nature.

MISCELLANEOUS

While BPD individuals certainly can have their share of dysfunctional thinking, it is also true that health care professionals can exhibit dysfunctional thinking toward BPD individuals as well. Although it seems to be improving, the bias toward this population is still hurtful to many. I have had many patients whose health care provider assumed they were lying, faking, or making up symptoms due to their diagnosis. The result is many patients don't get the medical care they legitimately need.

TIPS FOR THERAPISTS

Avoid "Should Statements." Cognitive distortions are not just for patients. Learning to be aware of these and challenging them appropriately can help anyone in any setting in life. This is also true for professionals dealing with emotionally dysregulated patients. "Should statements" may be the most important to guard against, as BPD individuals tend to frequently elicit them from professionals. Learning to identify and challenge your own *shoulds* toward your patients can be vital for working with these individuals in the most effective manner. Below are some common *shoulds* professionals may have toward BPD patients and some possible challenges that can keep you, as the therapist, regulated:

Health Care Worker *Should* Statements	Rational Responses
• She shouldn't be attention seeking • He shouldn't manipulate • She shouldn't have angry outbursts • He shouldn't cut himself like that • She shouldn't react so extremely when I tell her I'm going on vacation • He should learn from his mistakes • How can she make the same mistake over and over again? • She shouldn't be so needy	• Behaviors eliciting sympathetic responses are symptoms of the condition we are treating. It isn't rational for us to expect a diabetic not to have unstable blood sugar. It also isn't rational to expect BPD individuals not to engage in these behaviors. • If they already had these behaviors under control, they would not need my help/treatment. • Personality disorders are ego–syntonic. Learning from past experience takes much harder work for her than most. • She never got her needs met growing up. We all have needs. Picture her as that little girl not getting what she needed from her mother. Show some compassion.

Challenging *shoulds* is all about having appropriate expectations and demonstrating empathy. It is not reasonable for us to expect people to not exhibit the symptoms of the condition they are presenting for. Remember, even though there is an element of choice in these behaviors, these individuals don't want to be this way. Nobody wants to feel miserable. As we master challenging our distortions as health care professionals (and not just tell ourselves these challenges at some superficial level, but truly come to believe those challenges), work with this population becomes much more effective and rewarding for the clinician and the patient alike.

Don't personalize. Personalization is another common thought distortion for clinicians. Consider these common *personalizations* and possible challenges:

Personalizations of Health Care Staff	Rational Responses
• Since he isn't getting any better, it is my fault. • Since she hurt/killed herself, it is my fault.	• Maybe he is getting better slowly. • Progress is much slower with this diagnosis. Have realistic expectations. • Some people with BPD don't get better. If I am offering evidence-based treatment and they aren't complying with treatment recommendations, it is unfair to blame myself. • If a person decides they are going to hurt or kill themselves, that is ultimately their decision. Many times, nothing can be done to stop it. If I am practicing competently and acting in the best interest of the patient, I am doing my part. This is a two-way street.

An old adage a psychiatrist shared with me that he was taught was: "If the patient does not respond to the course of treatment, they must have a personality disorder. Don't worry about it. You have done everything you can do." While it is unfair and counterproductive to always blame the patient when desired outcomes are not achieved, there are times where this is appropriate. Patients have a shared responsibility in their progress. Treatment for BPD is not surgery. While it does involve expert knowledge, it is not the clinician doing something *to* the patient while the patient is unconscious. Effective treatment is a collaborative process in which both the health care professional and the patient must do their parts for treatment to be successful. If the therapy is unsuccessful, it isn't always the clinician's fault.

Observe limits. Setting and keeping limits is vital for providers as well as BPD patients. Be consistent with appointments. Do not run late. Follow treatment guidelines. Be clear with expectations at the outset of treatment. The harder you work to be clear about establishing expectations at the outset, the easier it will be throughout the course of treatment. If you do phone coaching as a component of therapy, have a clear contract of acceptable times to call, how long the sessions will last, and what will happen during the calls. Stick with the limits you set.

Get consultation. Some treatment models require therapist supervision/consultation. This is one of the four components of the DBT protocol. The reality is that regular consultation is not always practical, feasible, or available. Some clinicians need it more than others. Know your skill level. Regular consultation can be beneficial if you can get it set up. Even if you don't participate in regular consultation, seek it out for particular cases that are challenging for you. Not only is this a staple of professional ethics, it can greatly enhance your ability to work effectively with this population.

Take care of yourself. Many therapists are not good at taking their own advice in this area. Their self-sacrificing beliefs are so compelling that they are much better givers than receivers. They are much better at taking care of others than taking care of themselves. Self-care for us as health care providers is just as essential as it is for our patients. Have family time. Practice your faith. Cultivate your own hobbies. Create time in your schedule for you to not even think about your work setting so you can recharge. A "helper" whose gas tank is constantly running on empty is not very effective. With today's busy schedules and productivity expectations, this can be difficult. But be intentional about making this time for yourself. It will help prevent burnout, and will make life in this field much more fulfilling for you as well as for your clients.

CHAPTER 12
WHAT FRIENDS AND FAMILY NEED TO KNOW

What To Look For:

Does One of Your Loved Ones Have BPD?

- Does your loved one repeatedly accuse you of wanting to leave them or threaten to leave you?
- Does he/she get their feelings hurt routinely or feel rejected in response to things you say?
- Does your well-meaning constructive criticism fall on deaf ears and often provoke an escalation?
- Does your relationship with your loved one feel volatile? Do they praise you one moment and then quickly get angry with you before you know it?
- Are they frequently ending relationships for periods of time, only to take you back into their good graces later?
- Does your loved one at times express feeling completely unworthy to be with you, yet at times is enraged with you or seems to be attempting to control you?
- Do your attempts to resolve conflicts frequently result in intense, long conversations?
- A lot of people may seem "oversensitive," but does your loved one exhibit daily mood swings that can range from seemingly content, to extreme anger, anxiety, agitation, sadness with alarming rapidity?
- Does criticism make them feel horrible inside even if delivered from a caring place with constructive intent?
- Do they claim others can "make them feel" a certain way?
- Does your relationship seem to be intense, chaotic, and to take more energy than those of others you observe?

If several of these describe your relationship with your loved one, it is likely they have Borderline Personality Disorder or BPD traits.

BPD AND THE FAMILY

It is often not easy to find help caring for a loved one with BPD. Resources exist, but their numbers pale in comparison to those available for other conditions. BPD affects family members in numerous ways. Family members often *feel* manipulated, although often that is not the intent of the BPD individual. For example, "guilt stabs" are a frequent weapon in communication, which leaves some family members paralyzed and feeling trapped in a double bind. It is important to note that these behaviors are often attempts to gain validation.

Well-meaning people don't know how to respond. Usually vicious cycles start early in development. Dysregulated babies can produce invalidating responses. Parents, especially young moms and other ill-equipped parents, are more prone to be reactive in harmful ways to children who – by temperament – are unhappy. Some parents are overly concerned with image, and what the community thinks. Some parents do the best they can. But, as the child continues to develop, the cycle continues to perpetuate. As these children grow, their parents often feel helpless while watching their BPD children engage in various types of self-destructive and self-sabotaging behaviors. Attempts to help are often perceived as "controlling." Not helping may be perceived as "not caring." Many parents become overinvolved, thus escalating the conflict. Others give up and become distant, which continues to be perceived as "uncaring."

Siblings of BPD individuals are often affected. It is not an uncommon experience that one is pulled into the care-taking role. Some siblings also become the "good child" in the eyes of the parent, which fosters devaluing and resentment from the BPD sibling. So, by no fault of their own (sometimes), they become an object of hate (although, sometimes they contribute to it).

BPD can often have harmful effects on extended family. Due to inadequate or irresponsible parents, grandparents, aunts, uncles, and other relatives are often pulled in to help and they can also feel the stress involved with caring for an individual with BPD.

If your parent has BPD, you may feel deeply hurt and frustrated by their behavior. Some may have spent much energy in an attempt to win their approval – they constantly rejected you, so you were never good enough. Some children of BPDs grew up in chaotic homes. Some were more neglected by dissociated or absent parents.

Many people in dating or marital relationships with individuals with BPD feel as if they are the crazy ones. One of the criteria for BPD in the DSM-5 is a "pattern of intense and unstable relationships," and this most often manifests in the context of romantic relationships. People with Borderline Personality Disorder tend to blame, attack, "guilt stab", threaten, or verbally assault during episodes. Usually they feel awful after they have calmed down because this does not reflect their true character. Emotional outbursts "out of left field" are common. It is important to remember that these are affected by the BPD individual's perception to the event or statement preceding the outburst.

Perception has to do with the way one views incoming information. Perhaps you have heard the definition of communication as "a message sent plus a message received." The core beliefs of the BPD individual filter the "information received" in such a way that the BPD individual hears something different than what was intended. Note the following interaction from a couple's session:

> **Therapist to boyfriend:** "Thanks for coming to be a part of this session. I was slightly worried you would not make it. Did you find the place OK?"
>
> **Boyfriend states to therapist in front of BPD girlfriend:** "Yes. I found it fine. It is a long way across town from my office, so I was five minutes late. I apologize."
>
> **BPD girlfriend's belief: (filter)** "I am worthless."
>
> **BPD girlfriend hears (her perception):** "How dare he not think I am worth driving this far for!"

The BPD girlfriend now feels hurt and angry before the session even begins, which further increases the boyfriend's perception that nothing will work.

The boyfriend was simply answering the therapist's question, with a very brief comment accounting for why he was five minutes late. In actuality, the boyfriend just wanted the therapist to know that he was slightly late because of the distance he had to travel over lunch hour traffic and not because he did not value the appointment. The BPD girlfriend's filter heard something that was never intended. So these meltdowns that may appear to be "out of left field" are never out of left field. There is ALWAYS a trigger related to something that has just happened or was just said.

With this in mind, here are a few keys for communication with someone with BPD:

- Openness and good communication are essential.
- Communicate clearly what you mean – with your loved one's filter in mind.
- If and when miscommunication happens, restate your position *clarifying your intent.* It can be helpful for either party in a discussion to calmly state "Here is what I heard. What did you really mean by that?"
- Avoid "mind reading." As well as you may know your loved one, you don't always know what they are thinking. Ask them.
- Provide a "blame free zone" – give room for mistakes.
- Judge your BPD partner's progress *fairly.* If he/she is improving in certain areas, notice those and give credit for the improvement.
- Provide yourself with evidence reminders that your partner loves you. 3x5 cards can come in handy during times of uncertainty.
- Take responsibility for your part. If you are partially to blame for an argument, acknowledge it. Owning up to your part can go a long way toward healing in the relationship.
- Set boundaries. Recognizing progress and validating emotions does not mean tolerating abusive behaviors. If these occur, refuse to tolerate them. Call in a third party. Leave if necessary.
- Take care of yourself. It is important to have friends and interests outside of the relationship. Good self-care is important for both partners.

FAQ/WHAT FRIENDS AND FAMILY MEMBERS NEED TO KNOW

Is lying a symptom of BPD?

Because distorted beliefs cloud their perceptions, individuals with BPD will often view things differently. This does not mean they are *lying*. Lying is *intentionally* telling an untruth. It is true that their perceptions of reality will sometimes be off, but it is never helpful to call them liars or perceive them as that. It usually isn't true.

Are people with BPD abusive or violent?

There is evidence that men and women who have committed violent acts have elevated rates of BPD compared to the general population. However, it is important to recognize many with BPD are not violent at all. Impulsivity is one criterion and violent behavior is just one manifestation of that. People with BPD often experience intense emotions and rage is one of those, but the majority of people with BPD are rarely, if ever, violent.

Is manipulation a symptom of BPD?

Many people in relationships with BPD individuals will report *feeling* manipulated. The "push-pull" dynamic of the borderline relationship is sometimes responsible for this. As noted in the self-harm criterion section, one of the motivations for parasuicidal behavior is to elicit a sympathetic response. While it is true that the BPD individual often engages in indirect validation-seeking behaviors rather than communicating those needs directly, manipulation, to the degree that it exists, usually does not serve the function believed.

Are people with BPD irresponsible?

All people with BPD are not the same. Some of my BPD patients are the most reliable and responsible patients that I have ever had. I have many that never miss an appointment and never miss a group. But others, for various reasons related to the disorder (although it should be noted that many non-BPDs can be unreliable as well) may exhibit irresponsibility. One reason may be due to the constant chaos in many of their lives. Things "come up" that take precedence in their minds. These may be related to consequences of their erratic behavior. Sometimes they may be related to the behavior of family or those close to them. Sometimes intense emotions influence them from keeping responsibilities. For others, dissociation may cause them to lose track of time and not realize they missed an appointment or personal commitment.

Are they incapable of understanding or caring? Will I ever get my needs met?

The answer to many of these questions is the same: All people with BPD are not alike in all ways. Most people with BPD can be very caring, although they are not that way 100% of the time. The reality is none of us are that way 100% of the time. However, individuals with BPD can be quite inconsistent with their ability to meet the needs of others they are in relationships with. They may appear unwilling. Even though people with BPD can be passionate and fun and spontaneous at times, at a deeper level, they don't have much self to give. Get your needs met elsewhere. Self-care is vital for those in relationships with individuals with BPD. The more you take care of yourself, the better chances you have of having a meaningful relationship with them.

People with BPD usually look OK – are they faking?

Many people with BPD have excellent social skills on the surface. It is only when relationships get intimate and they have difficulty handling the closeness that things can get volatile. BPD is in some ways a silent disease. People can look "fine" on the outside, but can be experiencing deep pain on the inside. Having BPD does mean that daily life proves more difficult for them and it is important to know they are genuinely suffering.

Are they all needy?

Many people with BPD do come across as "needy." This again is a manifestation of the abandonment criterion. People with BPD have different coping styles, so they may manifest the fear differently, but the majority of them cope in ways that, "do everything within my power to know that you are there for me and that I am not alone and will not be left." So multiple phone calls, constantly needing someone with them, and smothering behaviors are common in BPD. Some may actually fear you will cut them out of your life without warning. In these times of fear, they will seem more clingy, needy, irritable, or far too willing to please.

Do borderlines always have bad parents?

Remember, there is a strong genetic component to BPD. While many with this disorder had invalidating family backgrounds of some kind, it is not always accurate to blame the family. Even in cases where the family has contributed, casting blame is rarely helpful in finding solutions and leading people toward recovery.

Do they really just go off for no reason?

Extreme mood shifts are common in BPD. Forming and maintaining relationships is a struggle for every individual with BPD. They can be very extreme or rigid in beliefs, choices, and behaviors. Middle ground can be difficult to comprehend. But it is *never* "for no reason." See the section above on the role of perception in BPD. There is always a reason. The reason may not seem logical to the family member, but there is always an environmental trigger that makes sense to the BPD individual.

Do all borderlines cut? Are all cutters borderlines?

The answers to these questions are NO and NO. Twenty to twenty-five percent of individuals with BPD will never perform a self-damaging act. Not all people with BPD have thoughts of self-harming. Of those who do, not all act on those thoughts. Self-injurious behavior is common in individuals with BPD (although it should be noted that not all self-injurious behavior involves cutting), but there is a percentage of individuals who never will.

On the flip side, cutting has almost become a fad in some parts of the United States. The vast majority of these cutters are girls, but the *New York Times* published an article recently highlighting fad cutting increasing in teenage boys as well. So just because a teen may begin cutting does not automatically mean they are a "budding borderline." Get them to a qualified mental health provider to help understand the motive behind the behavior and related diagnostic evaluation.

Should I always assume they are attention-seeking?

I have actually heard nursing and social work programs teaching this. This is ineffective management of BPD at best and harm-causing at worst. As highlighted earlier in this book, there are about eight motivations endorsed for self-injurious behavior – only one of which is related to eliciting a sympathetic response ("attention-seeking"). So not only is assuming that all self-harming gestures are attention-seeking usually inaccurate, it sometimes does the borderline patient harm. Often this will just trigger BPD individuals to "up the ante" and do something more dangerous. Never assume you know the motive. Work to get to know your loved one. Participate in their treatment. Understand the function of their behaviors, and learn to act in ways that support that individual's recovery.

I've heard people with BPD are incapable of insight? Is this true?

Due to the ego-syntonic nature of BPD, insight is difficult for many of these individuals. However, as with any condition, one can have a "mild" version, a "moderate" case, or more "severe" manifestations. Those on the mild to moderate end of the spectrum tend to have better insight. Insight can be gained over time. Even though this is not an area of strength, it does not mean it is not an area that can't be improved upon. So don't give up!

Do individuals with BPD get involved with the legal system?

Due to impulsivity, individuals with BPD often make decisions without regard for consequences. Occasionally, this may involve aggression, stealing, shoplifting, etc. – so, occasionally, individuals with BPD can have some legal concerns, but these are not frequent occurrences. They are more likely to have issues involving cannabis or other substances.

Is substance abuse a symptom of BPD?

Co-occurring rates of alcoholism and other substance use disorders are remarkably high in this population. Many people with BPD engage in substance use as a means of not having to feel the intense emotions they so often struggle with. Many will state, "I just didn't want to have to think about all this for a while." It is noteworthy that a decent percentage of individuals in substance treatment programs will report having a "substance of choice." Very few individuals with BPD will report having a substance of choice. This just seems to be yet another manifestation of the impulsivity phenomenon. Substance use may simply be one of many behaviors people try in an attempt to not have to feel something they'd rather not feel.

Are borderlines hypochondriacs?

Many individuals with BPD have legitimate health concerns, and this disorder can also have an impact on physical health issues. BPD has been associated with a variety of health conditions such as chronic pain, fibromyalgia, obesity, arthritis, diabetes, and others. Additionally, long-term effects of self-injurious behaviors or eating disorder behaviors can have long-term health effects as well. While some people with BPD will exhibit somatic symptoms (physiological symptoms with no identifiable medical origin), medical treatment should always be sought to rule out actual physical issues. It is worth pointing out that it was once believed that 90% of impotence was psychological. We now know that 90% is physiological. A number of other examples could be highlighted to point out that many symptoms that were once believed to be "somatic" ended up being related to a "legitimate" medical problem science simply did not yet understand. Support your loved one's medical needs. Only after multiple medical and psychological providers have suggested the possibility, should a somatic origin be considered.

Is shock treatment helpful for people with BPD?

The impulsivity criterion in chapter one highlights the phenomenon of individuals with BPD regularly looking for the quick fix. For this same reason, many individuals with BPD have been on multiple medications, which rarely have more than a minimal effect. When these fail, many with BPD will continue their search for external solutions to change their undesirable internal states. Thus, natural remedies, biofeedback, EMDR, acupuncture and electroconvulsive therapies are often sought. I even had one patient try a New Age crystal worship healer! This just provides another opportunity to reinforce that psychotherapy that teaches the BPD individual skills to learn to regulate their own internal emotions is the only way to truly develop some freedom from these intense feelings and resulting behaviors that make things worse. Beware of and resist the temptation to go on a wild goose chase seeking the external miracle cure.

Are there online support groups?

BPD individuals supporting other BPD individuals is a double-edged sword. There is a thin line between validation and stirring the pot. On one hand, many people with BPD enjoy feedback from others who they often believe are the only ones who can really understand what they experience. And there is much value in this. However, because they are prone to the same types of dysfunctional thinking, they can also fuel each other's distortions and encourage similar ineffective behaviors. Also, calling each other in times of crisis can present a number of challenges. The BPD individual called upon may not be in a stable enough place emotionally to be able to offer the help that is needed. Many individuals with BPD are prone to unhealthy guilt, which often places a false sense of responsibility on the person on the receiving end to make sure the other is safe. Finally, because people with BPD, in general, are much more prone to have their moods affected by the ones around them, dealing with another's crisis is often extremely stressful to them.

There are additional risks associated with online support groups. You don't really know the people you are supporting and being supported by (although many with BPD will *feel* like they do). You are not there to be able to help them in person. You don't know their crisis information and they don't know yours. Additionally, there are a number of rather sick BPD chatrooms out there that can fuel intense emotions in harmful ways. Also, due to the multiple manifestations of BPD discussed earlier in this book, you may not be able to relate to what is being shared. Many of our patients find that online support/chat rooms are often filled with horror stories and worst case scenarios that actually don't relate to them at all. Occasionally, a person will find some comfort in an online support group that can help them work towards health and recovery.

If you choose to be a part of one of these groups, I would encourage you to give it a trial run. Run it by your therapist and one other person who you trust that knows you well. Seek their feedback on the effect it is having on you. The bottom line is anything that helps you move toward recovery could be healthy for you and worth doing more of. Anything that moves you away from recovery is unhealthy and wise to avoid. Remember, you may not have immediate insight as to how these are affecting you. Evaluate them the way you would any other tool. Use wise minds in your life to help you make the decision.

How can I help?

More on this later, but family members may be called upon to help ego-syntonic individuals in treatment. Be willing to participate as much as your loved one is comfortable with. Provide objective feedback. Help them notice mood swings and remind them of related behaviors used to cope with them. Understand their buttons. Be a part of and help them establish a dependable support team. Don't enable their unhealthy behaviors. If you are uncertain of the effect you are having on them, consult their therapist.

I have heard individuals with personality disorders are untreatable. Is this true? Is there any hope?

This was an unfortunate myth that persisted for many years. It is a myth we are still working to combat in the public's perception. As reviewed in the treatment section, we now have several effective treatments for BPD and most who apply themselves to the process get significantly better. The DSM–5 committee even went out of its way to issue a statement to combat the old erroneous notion; it stated, "contrary to the perception of many, prognosis for most people with BPD is actually quite good."

Treatment takes time (typically 1-5 years, depending upon the severity of the condition) and takes work. But most do make significant progress. Don't give up on them if they are working an evidence-based program.

WHAT NOT TO DO/SAY

"Get over it."   This sounds a bit harsh. But a lot of family members say things like this. "Pull yourself up by your bootstraps" is another favorite. People without BPD have often endured hard times in their lives, as well, and have coped with trials in spite of their feelings. This may just be a way of encouraging their BPD loved one, but it is always received poorly and perceived as invalidating.

"I understand."   This phrase is often well-meaning and is even taught in some "active listening" sections of counseling books. It is intended to convey an attempt to "hear" where a person is coming from. However, these words often elicit the thought in the BPD, "You do NOT understand what I have been through! How dare you say that you do!" This again underscores a LACK of understanding of what the BPD individual has been through, and in her mind, minimizing her emotional pain. One myth is that you must completely understand someone to know how to help them. Alcoholics Anonymous and other 12 step groups have actually perpetuated this myth with the idea that "to help an alcoholic you have to have been an alcoholic – you have to have been there." This is nonsense. Studies have actually shown (both with marriage counseling and addiction) that *personal experience* with something does NOT make one a better helper of someone else who has been there. It does help the individual feel more understood, but that does not translate into being the best helper. A more effective response is usually, "You are right – I have no idea what it is like to experience what you have, but I'd like to help you anyway. Help me understand what I can do to help you."

"You look so normal."   This is frustrating for many with BPD. The BPD individual's pain is *unseen*, so the reality is that they suffer in silence most of their lives. So, for people to say things like, "You look so cute," or "You seem so smart," or variations of this are extremely invalidating. As alluded to earlier in the book, many people with BPD self-harm for this very reason: to externalize internal pain. . . so others can see how badly they hurt. Avoid comments of what they look like on the outside at all costs.

"Please don't overreact again."   This will get the reaction you fear 10 times out of 10. This statement feels incredibly invalidating to the individual with BPD. In their mind it is not an overreaction. In their mind, their reaction *IS* justified and *IS* proportionate to what was just said. Don't minimize their experience, even if you do not understand it based upon what just happened from your perspective.

"I'm not the crazy one."   This one should go without saying. But unfortunately, it doesn't always. Diagnoses should never be used as a weapon. In addition to being the kinds of statements that make BPD individuals regret having trusted you with information about them in the first place, it often isn't true! Research shows that BPD to some extent runs in families. It also shows that we consistently date or marry people who are just about as emotionally healthy as we are! So oftentimes, people in the lives of individuals with BPD have their own dysfunction as well. It may be a different *type* of dysfunction, that might not have that particular label, but it is "crazy" nonetheless. Name-calling, labelling and blame-shifting are not helpful.

WHAT TO DO: WHAT THEY REALLY NEED FROM YOU

Unconditional acceptance – Accept them as a person. This does not mean condoning all behaviors. It is possible to show unconditional acceptance and valuing of the person while still disagreeing with behaviors. Communicate daily with your actions and your words that you value them as human being.

Consistency – Routine is helpful. Provide order when possible. Do what you say you will do. Demonstrate stability. Do not say one thing and do another.

Patience – Give permission to make mistakes. Everyone makes mistakes. Many people with BPD are working hard at recovery. Realize this is not a simple choice to change a behavior. Recovery is a long process that takes work. Just because your loved one still exhibits the behavior from time to time does not mean they are not improving. Family members have often come to expect certain unhealthy behaviors so they are *looking* for them. Rather than noticing and validating the nine times the person learned to hold their words, the family member will continue to point out the time that they yelled.

Dependability – Be a person they can depend on. Few others have been. In the long run, it is more helpful for them to have a consistent reliable person in their life who is there for them 70% of the time over many years than someone who is 100% there for a period of time but gets burned and backs out.

Trust – Trust is earned. Some people with BPD have behaved in ways that have contributed to lost trust. But *IF* your loved one is honestly working to earn it back, if you want the relationship to be restored, give them that chance. Resentments can NOT dissipate if relationships are not given the chance to heal.

Empathy – Empathy is tough for a lot of people. Empathy involves putting yourself in someone else's shoes and making an attempt to see where they are coming from. It does not mean you have to understand exactly what their experience is. That is impossible for those who have had different types of experiences. But make an attempt to feel the pain behind their words. Remember a time when you were in pain. Remember a time that you felt your worst. Your loved one may feel like that on a regular basis. Even though you may not know exactly how they feel, you know what it is like to be upset. Think of your most emotionally distressing moment – whether you were panic stricken, overwhelmed, or deeply saddened over a loss or personal betrayal. This is the type of intense emotion people with BPD feel on a daily basis. Putting yourself in their shoes does NOT mean it is best for you to condone their unhealthy behavior. But a little empathy can go a long way toward not harboring resentment toward them for their destructive behavior and can help maintain a working relationship.

Validation – It is important for family and friends to realize that it is possible to validate feelings without agreeing with interpretation of facts. Validation does not mean you have to agree with them. It simply means communicating to them that their feelings matter and their opinion counts. It is also possible to validate emotions without giving in to demands or "guilt stabs." Don't send them the message that to manipulate is the way to get what they want. Make every effort to reinforce healthy messages. Nobody likes to be manipulated. Encourage them not to treat people in ways that will cause them to resent them and reinforce their beliefs about others. Just let them know that they are not being dismissed and their feelings are valid whether you agree with their interpretation of the facts or not.

Honesty – Be honest. Do not lie to your loved one because you do not think they can handle the truth. If you need time to think about how to say what you have to say, tell them you will get back with them. Timing can be important. How you say what you say is very important. Word selection and tone of voice make a big difference in how a message is received. But don't lie to them and don't make decisions for them.

Communicate honestly and assertively. Set boundaries when needed. "I love you, but I am unwilling to do this," is much more effective than lying about something or not broaching a subject at all. After you calmly but assertively tell them "no" and stick with it, behave as though you care about them. It is actually better for you also to be firm but kind and tell them "no" when you believe you need to than to say "yes" to pacify them and then resent them for it later.

Someone to listen – Many times your loved one may just need someone to listen. It can be easy to be tempted to jump in and give advice. Just listen. If you have feedback, ask their permission to give it. "Are you interested in hearing my thoughts on it?" If they are not and you offer it anyway (especially in a scolding or demeaning way), at best, it will not be heard and at worst, it will trigger more intense conflict.

Personal space – Sometimes what your loved one may need most from you is space. As long as they have committed to be safe, do not chase them down. This only escalates the situation. Many loved ones get in power struggles. "She will not get away with this – she will answer me now" is the thought process of some as they chase their BPD loved one down the hall. Do not insist on "finishing this now." Although it is important to reach resolution on disagreements, the heat of the moment is not a time to force discussions of this nature.

Shared responsibility – Just because your loved one has BPD does not mean they are always 100% to blame in disagreements. Sometimes their BPD may have contributed to a misinterpretation or poor communication, but family members may respond to that in ways that they are also *partially* responsible for the altercation. Also, just because your loved one has BPD does not mean he or she is always involved in a problematic interaction. One of the most unhelpful things friends and family members can do is to always blame the BPD individual for relational issues and not take responsibility for their part in the problematic interaction or relationship. "She has BPD, so it is her perception that is responsible for this argument," is unfortunately often used. Always blaming their condition for a disagreement is 1) not fair or accurate and 2) counterproductive for your relationship. Many will regret they even gave you the privilege of knowing what their diagnosis was in the first place if it is used against them. While BPD perceptions do contribute to much relational instability, own your part. It will make life much better for all involved.

WHAT TO DO IN A CRISIS

Do not ignore threats of harm. Some nursing programs around the country actually teach students to ignore this behavior and it will go away. This shows lack of understanding of the BPD diagnosis and is certainly a bad idea. Often, this will trigger an escalation in the individual. "They don't see my pain, so I'll up the ante," and destructive behavior follows. It is unfortunate, but even today many nurses and other health care professionals are poorly educated in personality disorders. Validate emotions, set boundaries if necessary and contact mental health personnel if necessary.

Be familiar with and follow your loved one's safety plan. All individuals in treatment for BPD should have a safety plan. They should know their safety plan and have multiple copies of it. It is also beneficial for friends or family who are serving as members of the individual's support team to have a copy of the safety plan, so they can assist in a time of crisis. Know your loved one's treatment provider, crisis services (many outpatient providers are not available after hours) in the area and preferred hospital in case you need to call for evaluation. Have all these names and numbers in your phone or somewhere that can be easily accessed, as crises are never planned. Do not be afraid to call. Many friends or family members respecting the wishes of their BPD loved one do not call soon enough or never call at all for fear it will be upsetting to them. If in doubt, call. If you have been and continue to be a dependable person in the BPD individual's life, they will get over it. It is much better to act in the interest of their safety in an uncertain moment, even if against their will, than to not act to appease them and regret it later.

Do not allow threats. Any threat should be responded to with a call to an authority. Allowing them to hold you hostage is not good for either of you.

If a decision has been made to hospitalize, allow emergency services to transport rather than driving the person yourself. Many accidents occur during transports by non-emergency personnel. Ambulance or related services may seem unnecessary, but it is better to be safe than sorry.

If the individual is self-injuring, get in touch with your loved one's therapist or crisis resources after hours. It is true that parasuicidal behaviors are different than behaviors with suicidal intent, but let the professionals make that decision.

You may be familiar with a self-help resource on BPD published a number of years ago entitled *Stop Walking on Eggshells* (Mason, 1998). Two lovely ladies I know who struggle with BPD wrote this response. I thought it might be beneficial for you to hear, and I wanted to close this chapter by sharing their perspective.

What "walking on eggshells" means from a BPD perspective:

I, too, "walk on eggshells." Based on misconceptions born of gross generalities regarding the BPD diagnosis, family, friends, and especially professionals unfairly present me with biased expectations upon learning my diagnosis. From the moment my diagnosis is revealed, suddenly every action and decision I make becomes suspect. I quickly discover that I am disbelieved and accused of lying or being manipulative, resulting in a host of undeserved consequences: loss of relationships, providers refusing to treat me, inadequate and/or inappropriate medical treatment, being abused/assaulted/taken advantage of, ill-advised and unnecessary psychiatric hospitalizations, legal bias in cases ranging from civil to criminal, false accusations of abuse, being blamed for my illnesses—both medical and mental, and being "guilted" into situations in which I do not wish to be.

Mental and medical healthcare professionals can be quick to blame me for situations in which I did not participate or create, referring to my symptoms as "attention- or medication-seeking" or "controlling." Likewise, when problems arise in family and friendships, I find the blame is easily shifted onto me due to my BPD diagnosis and the popular misconceptions associated with it. If and when anyone at work learns my diagnosis, I sometimes become the company scapegoat. Authority figures rarely question the integrity of a non-mentally-ill person, but they quite regularly disregard a mentally-ill person, especially those of us labeled "borderline/ schizophrenic/bipolar," making life even more traumatic, scary, and difficult. All of these interactions influence my illness, and rest assured, BPD is not a choice.

Further, it proves difficult and disheartening to focus on positives in my life when those around me expect the worst from me, gossip about me, unjustly blame me, question my motives, and/or require verification of my actions. I am not saying that I am always or completely innocent, nor am I saying that I am without responsibility and accountability. I am not, and I know it. I am not afraid of accepting responsibility or being held accountable for the things I have done; however, I am afraid of being unfairly judged based only on a label.

I need the benefit of the doubt, but the knowledge of my diagnosis often supersedes that benefit. For these reasons, I also "walk on eggshells," hoping that someone nonjudgmentally listens, hoping that nothing bad happens: no disagreements, no arguments, no confrontations, and no contradictions, hoping that I am not defined by my diagnosis so that when I walk into a room I find my diagnosis has preceded me. . . because I understand how easy it can be to blame me when I am only seen as "a borderline." The truth in relationships—be they personal or professional—is that we each affect the other. We must live, work, and heal together. We share responsibility in our relationship. We both have needs, dreams, goals, and emotions that can trip us up along the way. And yes, we both "walk on eggshells."

BIBLIOGRAPHY

For your convenience, you may download a PDF version of the handouts
in this book from our dedicated website: go.pesi.com/BPD

Aguirre, B. (2013). *Mindfulness for Borderline Personality Disorder: Relieve Your Suffering Using the Core Skill of Dialectical Behavior Therapy.* New Harbinger: Oakland.

Ameli, R. (2014). *25 Lessons in Mindfulness: Now Time for Healthy Living.* APA Publishing: Washington, D.C.

American Psychiatric Association. (2013). Diagnostic and Statistical Manual of Mental Disorders (5th Ed). Arlington, VA: American Psychiatric Publishing.

Antony, M. (1998). *When Perfect Isn't Good Enough: Strategies for Coping With Perfectionism.* New Harbinger: Oakland.

Antony, M. & Norton, P. (2015). *The Anti-Anxiety Workbook: Proven Strategies to Overcome Worry, Phobias, Panic, and Obsession. (2nd Ed).* Guildford: New York.

Bateman, A. & Fonagy, P. (2004). *Psychotherapy for Borderline Personality Disorder: Mentalization Based Treatment.* Oxford University Press: Oxford.

Bateman, A. & Fonagy, P. (2010). *Mentalization-Based Treatment for Borderline Personality Disorder. World Psychiatry. Feb 9 (1). 11-15.*

Beck, A.T. (1975). *Cognitive Therapy and the Emotional Disorders.* International Universities Press. Madison, CT.

Beck, A.T. (1999). *Prisoners of Hate: The Cognitive Basis of Anger, Hostility and Violence.* Harper Collins: New York.

Beck, A.T. & Freeman, A. (2014). *Cognitive Therapy of Personality Disorders (3rd Ed.).* Guilford: New York.

Beck, J. (2005). *Cognitive Therapy for Challenging Problems: What to do when the Basics Don't Work.* Guilford: New York.

Burns, D.D. (1990). *The Feeling Good Handbook.* Plume: New York.

Claiborn, J. (2001). *The Habit Change Workbook: How to Break Bad Habits and Form Good Ones.* New Harbinger: Oakland.

Comer, R.J. (1998). *Abnormal Psychology, 3rd Edition.* Freeman Press.

Dean, M. (2006). *Borderline Personality Disorder: The Latest Assessment and Treatment Strategies.* Dean Psych Press: Kansas City.

Dimeff, L. A., & Koerner, K. (2007). *Dialectical Behavior Therapy in Clinical Practice: Applications Across Disorders and Settings.* Guilford: New York.

Ellis, A. (1975). *A New Guide to Rational Living.* Wilshire Book Company.

Farrell, J. & Shaw, I. (2012). *Group Therapy for Borderline Personality Disorder: A Step-by-Step Manual with Patient Workbook.* Wiley-Blackwell.

Fox, D. (2014). *The Clinician's Guide to the Diagnosis and Treatment of Personality Disorders.* PESI Publishing and Media: Eau Claire, WI.

Friedel, R. (2004). *Borderline Personality Disorder Demystified: An Essential Guide for Understanding and Living with BPD.* Da Capo Press: Chicago.

Freeman, A. & Fusco, G. (2004). *Borderline Personality Disorder: A Patient's Guide to Taking Control.* W.W. Norton: New York.

Gates, A. (1995). *The Road to Recovery: A Step By Step Guide to a Balanced Life.* New Forms Press: Stillwater, OK.

Gunderson, J.G. & Hoffman, P.D. (2005). *Understanding and Treating Borderline Personality Disorder: A Guide for Professionals and Families.* American Psychiatric Association: Washington, D.C.

Gunderson, J. G. (2008). *Borderline Personality Disorder: A Clinical Guide.* American Psychiatric Association: Washington, D.C.

Hays, S.C., et al. (1999). *A Practical Guide to Acceptance and Commitment Therapy.* Springer: New York.

Kabat-Zinn, J. (1990). *Full Catastrophe Living: Using the Wisdom of Your Body and Mind to Face Stress, Pain, and Illness.* Dell: New York.

Kernberg, O. (1984). *Severe Personality Disorders: Psychotherapeutic Strategies.* Yale University Press.

Kreisman, J. & Straus, H. (2006). *Sometimes I act Crazy: Living with Borderline Personality Disorder.* Wiley: New York.

Layden, M., Newman, C., Freeman, A., & Morse, S. (1993). *Cognitive Therapy of Personality Disorder.* Simon & Shuster: Needham Heights, Mass.

Leahy, R. (2003). *Cognitive Therapy Techniques: A Practitioner's Guide.* Guilford: New York.

Linehan, M.M. (1993a). *Cognitive Behavioral Treatment of Borderline Personality Disorder.* Guilford: New York.

Linehan, M.M. (1993b). *Skills Training Manual for Treatment of Borderline Personality Disorder.* Guilford: New York.

Lester, G.W. (2005). *Borderline Personality Disorder: Treatment and Management That Works.* Cross Country Education.

Mason, P. T. (1998). *Stop Walking on Eggshells.* New Harbinger: Oakland.

McKay, M., Wood, J.C., & Brantly, J. (2007). *The Dialectical Behavior Therapy Skills Workbook: Practical DBT Exercises for Learning Mindfulness, Interpersonal Effectiveness Skills, Emotion Regulation, and Distress Tolerance.* New Harbinger: Oakland.

Oldham, John, M. (2104). *The American Psychiatric Publishing Textbook of Personality Disorders.* APA.

Pederson, L. (2012). *The Expanded Dialectical Behavior Therapy Workbook: Practical DBT for Self-Help, Individual and Group Treatment Settings.* PESI Publishing and Media: Eau Claire, WI.

Preston, J. (2006). *Integrative Treatment of Borderline Personality Disorder: Effective Symptom Focused Techniques Simplified for Private Practice.* New Harbinger: Oakland.

Paris, J. (2010). *Treatment of Borderline Personality Disorder: A Guide to Evidence-Based Practice.* Guilford: New York.

Prochaska, J. O., Norcross, J., & DiClemente, C. (2007). *Changing for Good: A Revolutionary Six-Stage Program for Overcoming Bad Habits and Moving your Life Positively Forward.* Harper Collins: New York.

Riggenbach, J. (2012). *The CBT Toolbox: A Workbook for Clients and Clinicians.* PESI Publishing and Media: Eau Claire, WI.

Robinson, D. (2005). *Disordered Personalities, (3rd Ed).* Rapid Psychler Press: London, Ontario, Canada.

Satcher, D. (1999). *Mental Health: A Report of the Surgeon General - Executive Summary.* Professional Psychology: Research and Practice.

Sokol, L. & Fox, M. (2009). *Think Confident, Be Confident: A Four-Step Program to Eliminate Doubt and Achieve Lifelong Self-Esteem.* Perigee Books.

Velasquez, M.M., Maurer, G.G., Crouch, C., and DiClemente, C.C. (2001). *Group Treatment for Substance Abuse: A Stages-of-Change Therapy Manual.* The Guilford Press: NewYork, NY.

Warren, R. (2002). *The Purpose Driven Life: What on Earth am I Here For?* Zondervan: Grand Rapids.

Young, J. & Klosko, J. (1994). *Reinventing Your Life: The Breakthrough Program to End Negative Behavior and Feel Great Again.* Plume: New York.

Young, J. (2006). *Schema Therapy: A Practitioners Guide* (2nd Ed). Guilford: New York.